COOKING Wild

Copyright, Ken Allen, 1986

All rights reserved. No part of this work may be reproduced or transmitted in any form by any means, electronic or mechanical, including photocpying and recording, or by any information storage or retrieval system, without permission in writing from the publisher, except by a reviewer who may quote brief passages for a review.

Published by Gannett Books, Guy Gannett Publishing Co., 390 Congress Street, Portland, Maine 04104.

First edition printed in the United States of America by Gannett Graphics, Augusta, Maine 04330.

Library of Congress Catalog Card # 85-080242   ISBN # 0-930096-53-3

Ken Allen

 Gannett Books

Guy Gannett Publishing Co.
Portland/Maine

Dedication

I dedicate this book to my wife, Marguerite Gingras Allen, my favorite cook. Her culinary expertise was invaluable.

Acknowledgements

Many people have helped me write this book.

In 1979, Harry Vanderweide, editor of the *Maine Sportsman*, saw a need for a cooking column in his publication, and asked me to write it. *Country Cooking* was an immediate success, more than I had dreamed possible. Since the column's beginning, folks from every corner of the United States have sent me letters, and often, they have mentioned how nice it would be to have a collection of my recipes in a book. Because of this encouragement from strangers, I was more than ready to write *Cooking Wild* when Allan Swenson, book editor from Gannett, approached me with the idea of a cook book. Since the nucleus of recipes in *Cooking Wild* have appeared in my cooking column, a special thanks goes to Harry Vanderweide for encouraging me to write about cooking, and also, to my readers for their loyal support.

Tom Carbone and Tom Shoener of the *Maine Department of Inland Fisheries and Wildlife* made it possible for me to use several photographs from the department's picture files, so a special note of appreciation goes to these two gentlemen and the DIF&W.

My father and mother also deserve thanks. My mother always encouraged me to cook, and they both taught me at a very young age that anyone could supplement his or her larder very well from the woods and water. I grew up eating squirrels, rabbits, grouse, dandelions, berries, fruits, and particulary, venison.

And, finally, a special thanks goes to all my aunts, uncles, cousins, and friends who generously gave me ideas and recipes for this book.

October scene. A bird dog, brace of pheasant, and traditional, classic double. Courtesy of Maine Department of Inland Fisheries and Wildlife.

Introduction

There is a subtle message in this book, a message so many Americans have forgotten. Every day, something dies to furnish us with nourishment to live. Those of us living close to the Earth know this concept, and know it well. For us, eating is never a mundane experience, but rather, an act of worship . . . a celebration touching our primordial soul.

So often, in my life, a food-gathering experience such as hunting, fishing, or gardening has a particular scene. It may be a grouse rocketing through poplars with a background of yellow leaves and electric-blue sky, an Atlantic salmon finning weakly on the surface, or a butternut squash growing faster than the other ones near it. If the grouse happens to intercept a string of well-aimed pellets, and falls to the ground, then I always feel a touch of sadness and regret, truly felt, but I also have an image of a candle-lit dinner of roasted grouse complemented by a good French Chablis. The side dish may be that very squash, the one that grew so fast to give it an identity, the one I watched for six to eight weeks, and then ate in one meal. The salmon is another tragedy, but salmon steaks poached in a court-bouillon ease the sadness. That is a big part of what this book is all about. . . .

There are two other aspects to this book—simplicity and substitution. The recipes are simplicity in themselves, even the gourmet ones that make meals take on epoch proportions. Also, throughout the book, I urge you to substitute ingredients, even the main ones like the meat itself. If you have no venison steaks, use a lean beef steak. If you have no bear roast, a pork roast will work as well. If the recipe calls for tarragon, and you happen to be like me, and hate the flavor of it, use something else . . . something you like. For instance, in my kitchen, poultry seasoning is a work-horse seasoning, used in everything from home-fries to grouse. Be creative. That's what real cooking is all about. It is a high art form. Learn the basic strokes, and then try to create a master piece. And, above all, have fun.

Eat, drink, and smile at the changing seasons. Each one has its own bounty. . . .

Ken Allen

Belgrade Lakes,
Maine
October, 1985

TABLE OF CONTENTS

Introduction

Chapter 1	A Way of Life	Page 1
Chapter 2	January	Page 13
Chapter 3	February	Page 27
Chapter 4	March	Page 41
Chapter 5	April	Page 55
Chapter 6	May	Page 69
Chapter 7	June	Page 83
Chapter 8	July	Page 97
Chapter 9	August	Page 113
Chapter 10	September	Page 127
Chapter 11	October	Page 143
Chapter 12	November	Page 161
Chapter 13	December	Page 175
Chapter 14	The Wheat Connection	Page 187

Chapter 1

"A Way of Life"

From the short, winter days of January until the dark, festive month the following December, North America's woods, fields, and water produce gourmet foods of bountiful proportions for everyone with the knowledge and initiative to collect them.

Many recipes in this book are for wild foods, but some are for treats fresh from the garden. A few are for foods from supermarkets, and fish shops, particularly the seafood section. The majority of all these epicurean delights, however, share one thing. They are seasonal.

Waiting for a seasonal food whets the appetite. No one can have fresh fiddleheads in January, or Maine scallops in July. Since unprocessed foods make any dish special, we must wait for them—whether we are rich or poor. A touch of humility.

One appeal to this way of life concerns something that transcends the palate. Days when Americans relied on barnyard chickens or wild game for meals have long since disappeared for the majority of folks. It is a long way from a slaughterhouse to a modern supermarket where unseen meat-cutters neatly package various cuts, best side up, on styrofoam trays covered with cellophane. Such sterile conditions have helped modern man forget one basic truth of the universe. Something must die for us to live. Hunting, fishing, gardening, and gathering wild foods keep us close enough to the earth to re-establish this concept. Eating and drinking, as it should be, then becomes *an act of worship*.

Something did die. A breaded-venison cutlet or poached salmon steak was once part of a living, breathing creature. A side dish of baked squash was once a tiny fruit on a vine that was carefully weeded during the summer. Creamed mushroom toast was once fungi growing freely in a damp, rich pasture. Even the wine to accompany nature's free bounties came from the living. This knowledge...truly felt...is humility, but at once, paradoxically, elevates the soul. Dining no longer can be mundane. It is indeed a celebration.

A growing population with its inevitable by-product of development has put pressure on living off the land. No one would doubt that. But, on a positive note, there are more foods today than in 1620. Many edible wild plants thriving across this continent came from the Old World. Immigrants brought them for food or even decoration. These plants escaped domesticity and flourished in the wild. Purslane and Japanese knotweed are two perfect examples.

Some wildlife has not fared well since the Pilgrims landed, but many animals; white-tail deer and Canada geese are two dramatic examples, are more plentiful today than during the days of the Plymouth settlement. Brown trout and ring-necked pheasant were unheard of in the North American wild 350 years ago. Today, they are rather common in an outdoorsman's larder.

Food is there, free for the taking. Because of freshness and of absence of preservatives or dyes, it is more healthful. These are good reasons for spending a lifetime in the wilds, gathering food, but the real excuse is enjoyment. So, many days afield are the stuff dreams are made of...

All the recipes in this book are personal favorites. There is no hodgepodge of untried ones to fill pages. Some are exotic, and may be new. Many just strive to *perfect* old favorites.

Many fine folks look for recipes that would challenge the chef in an elegant restaurant, but never perfect simple ones like broiling steak, making gravy, or even scrambling eggs. All food has an easy trick or two to master. Learning them can make you a cooking legend, at least in your own family where it really counts.

Wild foods are less forgiving than blander, domestic edibles; consequently, they need extra care. It is worth it. The results will be food fit for the gods. The French Cooking School realized this centuries ago. The French long ago made game cookery a high art. They appreciated the delightful taste of nature's bounties.

Many of the recipes in this book are influenced by the French Cooking School. You will notice an absence of recipes calling for aluminum foil, browning bags, canned soups, or other paraphernalia so common in game recipes. You will see, over and over again, the recommendation to use cast-iron utensils, wooden spoons, crock pots, and whips. Certainly, part of this is aesthetic nostalgia, but a large part of this is quality, particularly with cast iron and crockery. They do work better.

Most of the recipes encourage creativity, particularly with substituting ingredients. In no place is that more evident than with the herbs and spices. For instance, if you dislike tarragon, use something else. If you have no thyme, feel free to substitute...instead of running off to the store. Many herbs and spices, particularly when fresh, have distinct flavors. Some, however, are quite similar. Recipes do not suffer, and just as importantly, can be tailored to a particular palate.

The temperature recommendations in the recipes are specific; the product of much experimentation. Stoves, particularly top-burners, vary greatly. If you have an electric stove, experiment until the results please you.

CAST-IRON UTENSILS

So often, dinner guests have praised our rice pilaf or mashed potatoes, rather simple dishes. Compliments are appreciated. Always. The praise, however, should go to the cooking utensil; not the cook. It is difficult to go wrong with cast-iron pots and pans, particularly with rice or potatoes. The finished product is always light and fluffy.

The even, constant heat of heavy cast iron enhances most foods. This relic from pre-Revolutionary War Days has qualities that newer alloys have yet to duplicate. Seasoned properly, cast iron is a snap to clean, and stews, soups, sauces, pot roasts, or what-not just plain taste better.

A cast-iron Dutch oven with a recessed cover and three legs is the most versatile utensil ever originated for open fires or fireplaces. The high sides allow safe frying, and any meal that may be prepared on a home range may be cooked over coals. You can even bake bread over an open fire with this utensil. After putting the bread pan in the oven, preferably on a trivet or three pebbles (this keeps the bottom from burning), set the Dutch oven on coals. Then, pile coals on the recessed cover, and the bread will bake. The finished product has a light, wonderful consistency unlike any other baking method. It could start a family tradition. Cakes, muffins, and pies also may be baked in this manner.

A thick, heavy, cast-iron griddle is excellent for pancakes. It also is superior for pan-broiling steaks. Because it has no sides, it does not lend itself to open fires, but on a range, griddles are hard to beat for these two foods.

Few country kitchens are without a cast-iron fry pan, and its virtues are legendary. Cast-iron pots, however, are less well-known, but should be in every kitchen. Vegetables come out so well in these pots. Besides perfect rice and potatoes, other veggies such as squash, carrots, parsnips, peas, string beans, and what-not benefit from even, constant heat.

A set of pots and fry pans in small, medium, and large size is a good start for outfitting a kitchen. The pots should be one-quart, two-quart, and three-quart sizes, and the fry pans should be approximately six, eight, and ten inches. A ten-inch griddle and a ten-inch Dutch oven with a recessed cover would complete the set. If the Dutch oven is for campfires or fireplaces, three legs on the bottom is ideal. If the oven is for a modern range, the model should be legless.

SEASONING CAST IRON

If cast iron is so great, why doesn't everyone use it? ...Simple. It requires more care and work than the newer alloys, but if someone exerts the effort, cast iron is worth the trouble. Properly seasoned, this material rivals teflon.

To season cast iron, fill it partially with oil, shortening, or lard, and place on a high heat. When this becomes smoking hot, reduce the temperature to low, and allow to sit for hours. You may want to occasionally scrape the bottom of the pan with a metal spatula. An old-timer once told us this smoothes the bottom and that's true.

Eventually, remove the utensil from the heat, and cool slowly. Pour the oil or fat out, and wipe with a paper towel. Ideally, this process is repeated every time the utensil is used, until there is no longer any sticking of food.

With new cast-iron utensils, it helps to cook foods that do not stick. For instance, you might want to start a new Dutch oven's life by cooking only french fries, nothing else for a period of time. A new fry pan may be used solely for bacon or Southern-style homefries. This is a fine way to season one perfectly. Sooner or later, a well-seasoned cast-iron utensil will be such a shiny black that you can see your face on the pan's bottom.

Pots are harder to season because they are used for boiling liquids. The chances are good that these utensils will never be seasoned as well as fry pans, but with age, they become remarkably efficient as far as not sticking. We have one that is used strictly for cheese or white sauce, and it barely sticks. A testament to age, and cast iron.

If someone makes something like stew or chile, it may stick, even when the utensil is properly seasoned. When this happens, a lot of fine folks claim soap and water should never touch the cast iron. That is narrow-minded.

Soap and water has its place, but we seldom use it. Our method is with salt. When food has stuck, we sprinkle salt into the utensil. The amount depends on the size of the job. Then, use a cloth or paper towel to rub the salt around the utensil. It absorbs the grease and scours the dried food away.

This is the old-time way of cleaning cast iron, but is not the only way. A good scouring of salt is as abrasive as steel wool, and also leaves a residue that may cause rusting, particularly in damp weather. After a salt scouring, it is essential to liberally wipe oil on the cast iron.

Soap and water are fine as long as no steel wool or similar abrasive is used. Dry and oil after washing, and the cast iron should be in fine shape. However, if it continues to stick, reseason. With age, this gets easier, and sticking becomes less and less of a problem.

Cast iron is tops. The new, shiny creations of the space age have yet to duplicate this ancient and honorable material.

KITCHEN TOOLS

A good roast is an epicurean delight. For perfect results every time, a meat thermometer is essential. Another thermometer for an inexperienced cook would measure the temperature of deep-frying fat. If cooking oil or fat is the proper temperature, the results will be perfection. Fish will be crisp and not greasy.

For stirring soups, stews, and what-not, it is hard to beat wooden spoons. They do not scrape the bottom of the pan. If someone has nice pots and pans, it is nice not to scratch them, but wood has another attraction. Some things like spaghetti sauce or chile tend to scorch on the bottom once in a while. If this scorched coating is scraped into the good sauce above, it will give it a burned taste. Wood stops this problem.

Wire whips are excellent for making smooth sauces or gravy. It is amazing how quickly a whip can smooth lumpy liquids. When buying one, remember: the more wire loops, the better.

One simple device that should be on the back of every stove is a camp salt shaker filled with flour. You know the style. It looks like a metal cup with a cover. This works very well for sprinkling flour into gravy, and sprinkles flour evenly on a bread board.

Heavy, crockery pots cook with a constant, even heat. A kitchen should have small, individual ones for Boeuf Bourguignon with Venison, or similar dishes. This makes any meal festive. A bean pot is great for making Coq au Vin, Jugged Hare, or Hasenpfeffer. In fact, cooking in an earthern crock is called "to jug." This stewing method is ancient and honorable, and tenderizes the toughest meats. Today, except for the recipe Jugged Hare, the term is obsolete. The result of "jugging" is so fine it should come back in style.

For yeast breads, a heavy, crock bowl is perfect; the heavier, the better. If hot water is run into the bowl before making the bread, the bowl will retain heat better. Temperature is crucial with yeast.

Sharp knives are essential for cooking. A well-equipped kitchen should have a French knife, butcher knife, boning knife, filet knife, and certainly, a paring knife. Once the investment is made in a set of quality knives, a superior sharpening stone (oil) and a sharpening steel are imperative to keep them razor sharp.

Sharpening a knife well takes practice and patience, but it is a skill worth learning. An oil stone with medium grit on one side, and fine on the other is perfect. Oil stones are superior to others because they resist breaking down, and do not load up as readily with steel filings.

For basting, a well-equipped kitchen should have three things. First, it should have a pastry brush used solely for basting water onto foods such as French bread. Basting bread while it bakes makes the crust "crusty." That is the secret to French bread. The second brush would be for basting barbecue sauce, etc. The third baster would be one of those giant "eye-dropper" gadgets. The end is inserted into the drippings in the pan below a roast, then the bulb on top is squeezed. This fills the plastic tube with hot drippings. Then, this liquid is squirted onto the roast. A marvelous kitchen aid for safe, efficient basting.

Wild meats tend to have more protein than domestic foods. Venison, for instance, has 40% more protein than beef. This sounds great until you realize it has 40% less fat. ...Great for the waist-line. However, it makes cooking a problem. Lean cuts dry considerably. Many recipes in this book call for wrapping salt pork, bacon, or pork fat around the cuts. This helps.

Back in pod-auger days, however, women larded their lean meats with a larding needle. This gadget helped them insert strips of fat into the meat. In those times, a larding needle was as common as a tea kettle. Now, you would be lucky to find one, but if you can, the results will be worth your trouble. Roasts will be mouth watering.

SUBSTITUTING MAIN INGREDIENTS

The bulk of recipes in this book are for wild fish and game; however, most of the recipes could easily be used for domestic foods. Venison recipes could use beef; grouse could be replaced by cornish hen; bear to pork; crayfish to shrimp; and the list can go on.

MAKING GRAVY

No two people make gravy that tastes exactly alike, but most folks follow similar rules-of-thumb. First, only two tablespoons of fat should be used for each cup of liquid. For thickening gravies and sauces, many recipes say to dissolve flour, cornstarch, or arrowroot before adding it to the hot pan of drippings. Good, solid advice! Many recipes in this book follow that routine. This helps insure there will be no lumps. This method, however, has one short-coming. The finished product tends to have a taste similar to the thickener. Because of this, it is a good idea to use this technique only for gravies or sauces with overpowering flavors.

When this is not the case, there is a different method for thickening. You cook the flour. This makes the thickener taste like the gravy instead of the other way around. Put the fat or melted butter in a heavy pan, and place on high heat. Sprinkle flour evenly on the bottom, and allow to brown. You may want to stir it a little. After it browns, turn the heat to low, then dribble in the liquid, stirring like crazy! After everything has been scraped from the pan's bottom, use a whip. Occasionally, there will be those dreadful lumps, but with practice, lump-free gravy, wonderfully flavored, will be the result time-after-time. The making of a legend!

When making a white sauce, melt the butter. As soon as it begins to bubble, sprinkle in the flour. When it begins to bubble again, stir. Watch carefully. Just before the flour begins to brown, remove from heat, and immediately dribble in cream or milk, stirring like crazy with a whip. Once the flour is dissolved, place back on the stove and continue to stir.

Each recipe in this book asking for gravies and sauces has explicit directions. Many of them are subtly different.

Flour and cornstarch make a clouded gravy. Arrowroot makes a beautiful clear gravy. Feel free in any of these recipes to switch from flour to the other two. Be creative, and enjoy.

GARLIC CLOVE COOKERY

Did you ever use garlic cloves and wonder why the garlic taste was bland? Isn't a garlic clove supposed to be enough to send anyone for a bottle of mouthwash?

Garlic cloves have an interesting characteristic. They must not be overcooked! If fresh garlic cloves are overcooked, the flavor is lost. Once a clove or cloves are minced or chopped, they should only be sauteed two to three minutes, no more. Any cooking time beyond that cooks away the garlic flavor.

Any place in this book that calls for garlic, garlic powder can be substituted for the real cloves. Cloves take a little extra effort, but it is worth it, particularly for family or friends.

CLEANING SMALL GAME

With small game, field-care is all-important. It begins with a clean kill. Ideally, the animal should be eviscerated as soon as possible, and the sooner they are skinned, the better. Scent glands should be removed, and then the carcass should be cooled; the quicker, the better. Running water may be needed to clean all blood and clots from the meat and bones.

Some folks like to soak small game in salted water for a night. Unless it is an especially tough, old animal with a strong smell, we don't bother. If the animal is going to be frozen, all pieces should be thoroughly dried with a paper towel. Then, wrap them in heavy-duty paper twice, and seal completely.

It is a good idea to parboil small game before cooking, but this depends on the recipe. In this book, any parboiling is explicitly stated; otherwise, no parboiling is necessary.

Everyone knows enough to age big-game animals, but a lot of people forget this precaution with small game. You need not age a squirrel or rabbit for a week. It might spoil! However, it is a good idea to leave small game in the refrigerator for 24 hours. It improves the taste immeasurably.

CLEANING UPLAND BIRDS

If God made a better food than grouse, we have yet to taste it. Because of this, we tend to be a little eccentric about preparation. For starters, a grouse should be eviscerated shortly after intercepting a string of well-aimed pellets. Preferably, a few seconds after it hits the ground.

If there is an apple tree handy, so much the better. A quartered apple should be stuck in the cavity, and then the bird should be cooled as quickly as possible. That is the key to all game preparation anyway. *Cool as quickly as humanly possible!*

Some folks skin grouse. The same ones put ice cubes in a glass of real French Chablis. Grouse should be carefully plucked. The finished product should look like a roasting chicken the week they are not on sale. In short, perfect.

Like any small game or fowl, make sure no clots or excess blood is left in the cavity before aging, cooking, or freezing. Do not be afraid to run water into the bird to clean it.

A night in the refrigerator is all the aging this bird needs. If it is going to be frozen, make sure it is wiped bone dry, and wrapped twice in heavy-duty freezing paper. If you plan to freeze grouse, do not bother to age them for 24 hours. Freezing and thawing serves this purpose well.

Pheasant and woodcock should be treated almost like grouse with these exceptions. It is nice to age pheasant two days. If the birds are going to be baked, a careful plucking job is the order of the day. They should be made as attractive and appetizing as possible, but just as importantly, the skin helps keep the flesh moist and succulent. Woodcock to be sauteed in butter, however, may be skinned. Early in the gunning season, pin feathers make woodcock skinning very practical. Immature birds do have pin feathers, and lots of 'em. Sauteeing woodcock keeps them moist, so the skin is not needed. Woodcock should be aged between 24 and 48 hours. This meat is very rich.

CLEANING WATERFOWL

Waterfowl should be eviscerated as soon as possible, then cooled quickly. Plucking or skinning depends on the species, and regional diet. Ducks such as teal, wood ducks, widgeons, pintails, and redheads should be plucked. Blacks, mallards, ringnecks, and canvasbacks usually should be plucked also. These ducks are the epitome of gourmet dining. However, the second group sometimes needs special care, depending on diet. It is seldom a problem. It is a good idea to pluck as soon as possible and age 24 to 48 hours, maybe a day longer for senior-citizen ducks.

Ducks that eat a fish diet should be skinned. This includes all the diving ducks. Dietary flavors are concentrated in the fat, so removing the skin and scraping off excess fat removes much of the offensive flavor. Then, wipe the bird with a cloth moistened with vinegar or lemon juice. Marinating sea ducks is also a fine idea.

CARE OF BIG-GAME

Care of big-game starts with a quick, humane kill. Then, the animal is eviscerated as soon as possible, certainly within a few minutes. Some hunters leave everything above the diaphragm until the animal is home. That is not a good idea. Everything should be taken from the cavity, and then the opening should be propped open with a stick. Like small game and birds, big-game should be cooled immediately.

Since quick cooling is essential, big-game should be skinned as soon as possible, even smaller big-game such as deer. If someone has a cool place with a constant temperature, you can't beat hanging an animal for one week. At the end of seven days, the meat looks dried out, but this is just a very thin layer on the outside.

In recent years, more and more folks take big-game to professional meat-cutters. Since self-sufficiency is so fulfilling, we hate to see this trend. With a sharp butcher knife, boning knife, meat saw, and meat cleaver, it is relatively simple to cut your own game up. By using a meat chart, a raw beginner can do a fine job.

When freezing big-game cuts, the same rules apply that were used for small-game and birds. Two layers of heavy-duty freezer paper tightly sealed is the secret.

CARE OF FISH

This is a concept easy to argue, but we do not use any water to clean fish. It seems to remove some of the natural juices in the flesh. Our real reason is simplicity. After scaling, the fish is wiped with a paper towel. This easily removes loose scales. After eviscerating, the blood sac along the backbone is easily removed also with a paper towel. Double the towel and press it with the thumb against the fish's backbone down near the anal opening. Wipe hard with the thumb, moving back toward the head, and the cavity comes clean as a whistle. What could be easier? Furthermore, the kitchen sink need not smell like fish for the next two days.

After killing a fish, the quicker it gets to the frying pan, the better. If this is impractical, get it on ice or refrigerated as soon as possible. Fish loses its freshness so quickly if the weather is warm.

As a general rule, if we are unable to get fish onto ice or into a refrigerator shortly after catching them, we throw them back for another day. Wicker creels look classy, but keep fish very poorly. The water-cooled canvas bags are infinitely better, but nothing beats ice or refrigeration.

No food loses its quality during freezing quicker than fish. The best way to freeze fish is in blocks of ice, and even then, plan to use it within a month or two. As a general rule, we never freeze fish, but are quick to admit this may be carrying things too far.

COOLING IN BROTH

When meat or fish is cooked in a liquid, it is a good idea to leave what is not used right in the cooking broth. If it cools in the broth, it will stay moist and succulent. If removed, it tends to dry out too much.

Along that same line, roasts should cool for 15 minutes before slicing; otherwise, juices will flow so freely from the cut that the meat will dry; 15 minutes is enough time so little juices are lost.

Following the foods through the seasons is a grand way of life. Bountiful days afield are truly the stuff of which dreams are made.

CLARIFIED BUTTER

Melt butter over medium-low heat, and then carefully skim foam from the top. You may want to cool the butter, reheat, and skim one or two more times. Then, pour liquid from pan, leaving sediments on the bottom. Clarified butter is less apt to scorch.

Chapter 2
January

January. The dark month so far from spring. Days lengthen, just a little, but few notice. Real cabin fever is weeks away, and indoors still feels good.

But outdoors we do venture. Some of us anyway. Snow makes fir thickets into fairylands of bowed limbs and endless tunnels, jeweled in sunlight. Alluring. Cross-country skiers and snowmobilers know this snow land. And so do rabbit hunters. Those white ghosts flitting through tunneled thickets and along alder edges beckon them. Year after year. January's inevitable thaw brings out that hearty, masochistic breed, the ice fishermen. A few pickerel and perch wind up on the ice. Rabbit, hare, pickerel, and perch. All delectable. Free for anyone willing to invest time, and a little initial money for equipment.

This is a grand month for cooking. Besides its fresh offerings for outdoorsmen willing to brave the elements, there should be some venison left in the freezer, usually tough cuts, challenging our culinary skills. Early sunsets give us plenty of time to fuss with meals that reach gourmet proportions, and mornings with the thermometer dipping below zero seem ideal for huge, leisurely breakfasts.

In many families, rabbit and hare are a traditional January meal. The holidays, with their festivities and confusion, are over, and time is set aside for running dogs in the country. Hopefully, a few rabbits will wind up in the game bag.

Europeans have long revered rabbit and hare, but in this country, except with hunters, few have tried this delightful food. It has a fine-textured consistency with a pleasant gamey flavor. Not strong at all.

When a food of the season first becomes available, people tend to use their favorite recipe. And we are no exception. The first rabbits of the year always end up as Jugged Hare. Jugged is almost an archaic term these days. It simply means to cook meat in an earthenware pot filled with liquid. It is a slow method of cooking, guaranteed to tenderize the toughest hare or rabbit.

JUGGED HARE

This is an ancient and honorable dish especially popular in merry olde England and Germany. Since the method calls for a rich, hearty wine sauce, it conjures up images of wealthy noblemen with their feet propped up on pillows, suffering from gout. It is a sinfully rich and delicious dish that may start a family tradition.

Jugged Hare has one excellent feature. There are no critical cooking times and ingredients and proportions may vary greatly. It is a democratic dish, nearly impossible to ruin. This makes it an excellent choice for company, especially since the preparations are mostly done three or four hours before mealtime. Gather the following ingredients:

- 1 cup flour
- 2 or 3 rabbits, cut in serving pieces
- 1–1½ cups of dry red wine
- 2 medium onions, quartered
- 3–4 cloves stuck in onion quarters
- 1 teaspoon salt
- ½ teaspoon pepper
- garlic powder
- chicken broth (enough to cover meat)
- mushrooms (optional)
- ⅓ cup of dry red wine (again)

After soaking the rabbit pieces in a solution of water and salt for a half hour, wipe with a paper towel and place in a bag. Pour most of the flour into the bag, saving three tablespoons for thickening the gravy later. Shake the bag vigorously, coating the pieces with flour.

Over a medium heat, brown the pieces in clarified butter or oil, then place them in the bean pot, alternating layers of rabbit with layers of quartered onions and the optional mushrooms. Fresh mushrooms are delightful, but canned will work. Whether you use sliced mushrooms or buttons is up to you. A democratic dish. Whatever suits the chef's whims....

Sprinkle in the pepper, salt, and two or three light shakes of garlic powder. Pour in the wine. Now, if you use chicken broth, make sure to boil it before adding it to the pot. If you cheat and use chicken bouillon cubes, it will be hot anyway. However, a word of caution with bouillon cubes. They are salty so go easy on the salt. Maybe just a third of a teaspoon.

Cover the bean pot and place in a 275° oven for three to four hours. Just before serving, remove the pot from the oven, place the pieces of rabbit on a warmed serving platter, then pour the liquid into a saucepan.

Bring to a boil, remove from heat, then slowly dribble in a paste made with three tablespoons of flour and enough water to make it smooth and somewhat runny. While dribbling the paste into the pot, stir like crazy with a whip. When all has been added, place back on stove over a moderately low heat and continue stirring until it begins to thicken. When the thickness suits your taste, thicken it a little more, then add one-third cup of dry red wine. This is a delightful touch, making it so rich. Pour this gravy over the pieces of jugged hare, and serve immediately.

French bread is a must with this meal. It adds a festive touch to a meal continental already. And, besides, there is plenty of gravy to sop up with the crusty French bread. Frenched string beans with slivered almonds or peas with pearled onions round this dish out. It is so rich and starchy no potatoes or rice are needed.

This meal calls for a good wine...red of course. It will complement a rich, somewhat heavy meal.

RABBIT STEW

Rabbit Stew is as American as apple pie and baseball. Rabbit and hare were plentiful and pioneers took advantage of them. Since one-pot meals were popular and easy in cast-iron Dutch ovens over open fires, rabbit stew was a mainstay.

Gather the following ingredients:

- 2–3 **rabbits, cut in serving pieces**
- 1 **large onion, chopped**
- 2 **chicken bouillon cubes**
- ¼ **teaspoon rosemary (optional)**
- ¼ **teaspoon thyme (optional)**
- **peas**
- **carrots**
- **potatoes (optional)**
- **mushrooms (optional)**
- **water**
- **salt and pepper**

Notice all the options! Another democratic dish. In a Dutch oven, preferably cast iron, add clarified butter or oil and place over medium heat. Add the rabbit pieces and chopped onions, and brown. If the pieces are dry, they brown better, so take a moment to dab them dry with a paper towel. If they are floured as in the *Jugged Hare* recipe, the pieces will brown even better.

When browned well, cover the pieces with water, and wait for a smiling boil. Then, add bouillon cubes, rosemary, thyme, and pepper. You may want to add salt. We don't. The cubes are salty enough. Simmer for one to one-and-a-half hours over a low heat. This tenderizes the toughest old bunny.

Remove the pieces from the Dutch oven and set them aside to cool. Make sure to save the broth. When cool, carefully bone the rabbit pieces, and put back into the pot with carrots, potatoes, peas, and mushrooms. The amount of veggies varies with the chef's whims. We plan on one to one-and-a-half cups of diced potatoes, a half cup of carrots, and a half cup of peas for each person. Maybe more! Reheated stew is superior fodder. Plan for leftovers. Cover the vegetables with broth and water, and cook until tender.

One option is adding peas 15 minutes before serving time so they do not overcook. We do this, feeling overcooked peas add little. Some folks like to cook a stew for hours; others take a chapter from the French cooking school and serve as soon as the vegetables become tender.

Before serving, thicken the broth with a flour paste made with three tablespoons of flour mixed with enough water to make it smooth and somewhat runny. Dribble this into the broth, stirring like crazy with a whip. If you remove the stew from the heat while performing this step, chances of a lumpy broth are lessened. When the paste has been added, place the Dutch oven back on a low heat and continue stirring.

Serve this meal with home-made biscuits, lots of butter, and hot tea or coffee. A hearty meal to revive anyone after braving the elements of a long winter's day afield.

RABBIT PIE

When we were young this was a favorite. Prepare a rabbit stew, leaving out the potatoes. You want very little thickened gravy if you use a pie crust. However, we make rabbit pie with a biscuit crust, and that absorbs lots of liquid, so you need a lot.

Pour the rabbit stew in a buttered casserole dish, or a deep glass pie plate. Cover with a pie crust or biscuit dough, and place in a preheated 400° oven until crust turns golden brown. With biscuits, this takes about 40 minutes, but keep a watchful eye.

FRIED RABBIT

As a kid, we seem to remember this was the most common way of cooking rabbit. Cut the rabbit(s) into serving pieces, then parboil for 30–45 minutes, depending on the toughness of the meat. It is too bad to parboil anything before frying it, but the procedure is essential to tenderize the meat. You may want to put an onion in the water while parboiling.

While it simmers, gather the following ingredients:

- ½ **cup flour**
- ¼ **teaspoon oregano**
- ½ **teaspoon poultry seasoning**
- 1 **egg**
- 1 **cup milk**
- 1 **teaspoon salt**
- **oil or clarified butter**

Put the flour, oregano, and poultry seasoning in a paper bag. Shake it to mix the dry ingredients. Pour the milk into a bowl. Add the egg and salt and beat thoroughly.

When the rabbit pieces are ready, remove from water, and let cool. Dip the cooled pieces into the milk and egg mixture, then drop into the paper bag. If there are a lot of pieces of rabbit, you will need to double or triple the flour mixture. When all the pieces are in the bag, shake vigorously, coating the pieces with flour.

Have ½ inch of oil or clarified butter heated to 375°. Place the pieces in the oil. Brown on one side. This should take no more than five minutes. Turn and brown the other side. Reduce the heat and cook 20–30 minutes. A medium-low heat works well for this last step. Watch it carefully. The flour and egg mixture tends to scorch easily.

Serve this meal with mashed potatoes, biscuits, and a green vegetable such as peas, string beans, or baby Lima beans. A cole slaw complements all of this.

FRICASSEED RABBIT

Fricasseeing is an excellent method of tenderizing rabbit, squirrel, or old chickens. Gather the following ingredients:

**2 or 3 rabbits cut into serving pieces
 1 cup flour
 1 teaspoon salt
 1 teaspoon poultry seasoning
 ½ teaspoon oregano
 ½ teaspoon pepper
 ¼ teaspoon garlic powder
 oil or clarified butter (About five tablespoons)
 water**

Put flour, salt, poultry seasoning, oregano, pepper, and garlic powder in a paper bag and shake vigorously. Next, in a cast-iron frying pan or Dutch oven, heat oil or clarified butter to 375°. When oil begins to reach this heat, place the pieces of rabbit in the bag and shake vigorously, coating the pieces. You may want to do only two or three pieces at a time. Drop the pieces gently into the oil and brown both sides. It takes about five minutes to a side. Reduce heat to low. After the pan begins to cool to a lower heat, add enough water to barely cover the meat, then cover the pan, and cook slowly. This can simmer for two, even three hours. We don't bother to thicken this broth. The flour on the meat thickens it a little anyway. This is an easy one-pot meal.

Mashed potatoes, buttered-parsleyed potatoes, or scalloped potatoes make an excellent accompaniment to this ancient and honorable dish. Biscuits seem a must with fricasseed anything!

This time of year, ice fishermen are catching pickerel, often big ones, and perch. No one would reasonably dispute the excellence of white perch. The meat is sweet and flaky. An epicurean delight. However, yellow perch need not be scorned, particularly this time of year. Yellow perch tend to be wormy in summer, but not in January. This fish is fine table fare.

Our first fish recipe this month is fish chowder. Pickerel and perch particularly lend themselves to chowder. They are boney, and since we bone the meat, we do not care.

FISH CHOWDER

We have a few secrets to good fish chowder. The two most important ones are using real heavy cream and not overcooking the fish. Also, a lot of fine folks begin fish chowder with salt pork. They sauté chopped onions with diced pork. This method has merits. However, we prefer to sauté the onions in butter.

This recipe calls for perch or pickerel, but any fish will do. Cusk, haddock, flounder, pollock, hornpout, sunfish, trout, salmon...all have their virtues. Fish chowder is another democratic dish!

Gather the following ingredients:

    water
    celery stalk, quartered lengthwise
    large onion, quartered
2 **pounds of fish, or more!**
2 **medium onions, chopped coarsely**
4 **tablespoons butter**
1 **teaspoon salt**
½ **teaspoon pepper**
    paprika (optional)
    parsley (optional)
¼ **teaspoon thyme (optional)**
1½ **potatoes per person**
½–1 **pint heavy cream**

Place the cleaned fish in a Dutch oven. Quarter a stalk of celery and an onion, and add them. You may want to sprinkle in a half teaspoon of salt. We don't. Put in enough cold water to barely cover the fish and place on medium heat. When the stock begins to simmer, reduce heat to low and watch carefully. As soon as the meat along the backbone turns from translucent to opaque—remove immediately from heat! Place the pieces of fish on a plate to cool, and save broth for chowder. It should be strained, removing the celery and onions. Discard this part of the broth.

When the fish has cooled, bone it thoroughly. In pod auger days, folks considered a bone in fish chowder sinful. Put the clear meat into the broth. Not overcooking fish makes the flesh moist and succulent. It is one of those small things that elevate cooks to legends.

Peel and dice potatoes into one-inch cubes. Cover with cold, lightly-salted water, and place on medium heat. Bring to a smiling boil, reduce heat, and let potatoes boil gently until tender. At this point, pour off the water, and place the pot back onto the heat for two or three minutes, shaking occasionally so potatoes will not stick. This makes the potatoes dry and fluffy, another plus in the making of a legend.

While the potatoes are cooking, take a Dutch oven, preferably cast iron, and melt the butter over a medium heat. Add chopped onions. You may want to sauté them until the pieces just turn translucent, or you may want to brown them. The degree of brown makes a big difference in the finished product. Dark brown onions make a richer chowder, subtly nutty. A lightly browned onion means a less rich chowder. It is up to the whims of the chef.

Now, add broth, fish, potatoes, salt, pepper, and thyme to the sautéed onions, and bring to a smiling boil. If you want a lot of broth, more water is needed. We dislike a soupy chowder. It is nice to have a little broth with a mountain of potatoes and fish in the center. Anyway, when the broth begins to roll, remove from heat and stir in the heavy cream. Place back on the heat and bring to a near boil. Be careful here. If it does boil, it will curdle. Very unappetizing. Remove from heat now. Ideally, this chowder should sit in the refrigerator for a few hours. It improves it dramatically. When ready to serve, sprinkle with paprika for color and garnish with parsley. Fish chowder goes superbly with biscuits and tea or coffee. Food fit for the gods.

January on the ice . . . trying to catch the makings of a fine meal. Photo courtesy of Maine Department of Inland Fisheries and Wildlife.

FRIED PERCH

Frying fish seems such a simple method, but it can drive inexperienced cooks into a closet! There are two ways it can go wrong. First, the oil has to be the right temperature—neither too hot, nor worse yet, too cool. Secondly, it is easy to overcook fried fish. Both mistakes cause unappetizing results.

When frying fish, we like to use a Dutch oven. Splattering is less of a problem. First, pour a quarter of an inch of oil into the Dutch oven or frying pan, and heat to 380°. A good way to hit this ideal heat is to place the burner on high until the oil bubbles. Reduce to medium and add the fish, being careful not to crowd the pieces.

While the oil is heating, dip the cleaned pieces of fish in milk and drop into a paper bag with a cup or so of flour, salt, and pepper. Shake the bag vigorously, coating the fish. Slide the fish gently into the pan or Dutch oven, and fry three to five minutes per side, depending on the size of fish.

This is where experience really counts. If you are unsure of the cooking time, after three minutes, lift a fish from the pan and gently flake the meat away from the bone on the cooked side. The ideal is to remove the fish just as soon as the flesh has turned from translucent to opaque. Serve with a lemon wedge, tarter sauce, boiled potatoes, and string beans.

BAKED PICKEREL

This time of year, big pickerel wind up on the ice. Big pickerel are ideal for baking. Eviscerate the fish, but do not remove the head, tail, or fins. This keeps juices from draining out during the baking process. Lay the fish on a baking sheet smeared liberally with butter. Stuff loosely with a bread stuffing identical to Poultry Bread Stuffing, and skewer the fish. Melt a stick of butter and lightly season it with garlic powder. You may want to put a half-teaspoon of tarragon and half-teaspoon of dill weed in the butter also. We do, but it's optional. This dish is simplicity in itself.

Baste the fish with this butter, salt and pepper it to taste, and put in a preheated 450° oven. Bake approximately 8–10 minutes per pound, basting occasionally. When the flesh along the backbone has turned from translucent to opaque, serve immediately. Buttered-parsleyed potatoes, string beans, French bread and a good white wine make this meal memorable. We might even splurge on a good French Chablis.

PICKEREL FISH CAKES

Let's face it. If you catch a bunch of small pickerel, you may fry them like perch; however, pickerel are notoriously boney. This recipe alleviates that problem. Place the cleaned pickerel in a Dutch oven, throw in a quartered onion, cover fish with water, and place on a medium heat. When it starts to boil, reduce heat, and simmer until the meat flakes easily from the backbone. Remove the Dutch oven from the heat, discard the broth, and lay the fish on a plate for cooling. When cool, bone thoroughly. For the recipe, you will need one cup of clear meat.

Now, gather the following ingredients:

- 1 cup of cooked fish
- 1 cup mashed potatoes
- 1 or 2 eggs, beaten
- 2 tablespoons butter, melted
- ½ teaspoon salt
- pepper to taste
- ¼ teaspoon dill weed (optional)
- ¼ teaspoon tarragon (optional)
- 1 finely chopped onion

Mix all these ingredients together. Make sure everything has been mixed thoroughly...no easy task. Form into balls or cakes. If you are deep frying them, balls are great. If you are using a frying pan, cakes are the thing.

Heat the oil until sizzling, about 380°, and add the balls or cakes. Brown and serve with tartar sauce, French fries, and cole slaw. A simple, cheap dinner fit for the gods. Cold beer complements this meal.

It's January. The glories of spring are a long way off, but January isn't half bad. It is a grand month for cooking and sipping good wine. Eat, drink, and smile. Spring will come. Eventually.

Chapter 3
February

February. Days lengthen. A little anyway. Astute observers of the natural world notice. Winter storms keep coming, and January's thaw is a distant memory. Snow is no longer a novelty. Just a drudgery, or joy. Hardwood ridges are deep with it and barren and so open you can see forever. But fir thickets are another thing, elfin, tunneled wonderlands, particularly after powder snows on a good crust, beckoning cross-country skiers and rabbit hunters with their hounds.

This is a glorious month for cooking. Nights are still long, ideal for preparing gourmet delights to share leisurely with bottles of wine and close friends brave enough to challenge a winter night's drive. Ice fishermen catch a few trout and salmon along with their perch and pickerel, and rabbit hunters add a few bunnies to the larder, but the real glories of this month come from tidal estuaries and the winter Atlantic! Salt-water smelts, sweet and delicate, run upstream to hopeful fishermen huddled in smelt shacks, and two of the world's most revered seafoods, scallops and shrimp, become available on the market. Halibut, another delightful seafood, are abundantly filling fishermen's nets. At no time are these three bounties from the sea more plentiful—or fresh!

COQUILLES ST. JACQUES

If Jugged Hare is always the way we prepare the year's first brace of bunnies, Coquilles St. Jacques is inevitably the method we use for the season's first pound of fresh scallops. This dish has tremendous snob appeal; however, the recipe is simplicity itself, and like many great French foods, has humble beginnings in cottages along the French coast.

This recipe is really Coquilles St. Jacques à Mornay. Mornay Sauce is a French cream sauce usually made with a combination of two cheeses. The word is usually left off because the dish always seems to be made with cheese anyway.

First, make a Mornay Sauce, but since timing is crucial with this dish, gather the following ingredients beforehand:

- 1 **pound scallops**
- 2 **tablespoons chopped onions, or shallots**
- 1 **teaspoon parsley (preferably fresh)**
- 2 **tablespoons butter**
- ¼ **cup dry white wine**
- ½ **cup Mornay Sauce**
- **buttered, dry bread crumbs**

Make sure the scallops are patted dry with a paper towel and the onions or shallots are chopped finely. With all the ingredients in place, you are ready for the Mornay Sauce.

Mornay Sauce

- 2 **tablespoons butter**
- 2 **tablespoons flour**
- **pinch of salt**
- **pinch of pepper**
- 1 **cup heavy cream**
- 5–6 **tablespoons (heaping) of Swiss or Cheddar cheese**

The secret to this sauce is to have it free of lumps. If you do it in the following way, there should be no problem. Melt butter in a small saucepan. Sprinkle in flour evenly. Stir constantly with a whip. When it first begins to bubble, remove from heat and add cream slowly, stirring constantly. Add the pinches of salt and pepper.

Place on low heat, and continue stirring. After about five minutes, it will begin to thicken. Add the cheese slowly, still stirring. We like a thick sauce because when we add it to the scallops with the wine and natural juices, the finished product may be too watery.

Once the sauce is done, back to the scallops. This part of the recipe takes crucial timing. Melt the butter over a medium heat until it just begins to bubble. Add the finely chopped onions or shallots immediately, and sauté for two or three minutes. Stir frequently. Make sure nothing browns. When the onions turn translucent, add the scallops. As soon as they begin to sizzle, cook for two to three minutes. Again, precise timing. Overcooking scallops just a little makes them tough and unappetizing. Next, add the wine. As soon as it begins to bubble, cook for 60 seconds. We say seconds instead of one minute just to emphasize the precise timing.

Add half the sauce, blend completely, remove from heat, and place scallops in four ramekins or a Pyrex pie plate. Liberally sprinkle bread crumbs on top and place under a broiler until the bread crumbs brown. This usually only takes a minute or so. Save the other half cup of cheese sauce for the vegetable served with this dish.

We always serve Coquilles St. Jacques with French bread, asparagus covered with the cheese sauce, rice pilaf, and French Chablis. It is such an eloquent meal we like to splurge shamelessly on the wine.

RICE PILAF

Rice pilaf goes with so many dishes, particularly gamey ones, but it really shines with Coquilles St. Jacques. First, gather the following ingredients:

    2 tablespoons butter
    1 large onion, finely chopped
    1 cup brown rice
    2 cups chicken broth
    ½ teaspoon salt
       dash pepper
       pinch garlic powder

One of our secrets to fluffy rice is a cast-iron Dutch oven. It makes such a difference. In a Dutch oven, put two tablespoons of butter and put on a medium heat. Add the finely chopped onion. In another pot, put two cups of chicken broth (we like 1 and 7/8 cups . . . it makes the rice delightfully firm . . . almost crunchy). Add a dash of pepper, a pinch of salt, and a pinch of garlic powder, and bring the broth to a roaring boil. While the broth heats, the onion begins to brown. The browner the onion, the richer the final dish. That subtle, nutty flavor of good pilaf comes from the browning of the onion. When the onion is browned, add the cup of rice and stir, coating the grains with the onion-flavored butter. Add the boiling chicken broth. The rice and broth should begin to boil immediately. As soon as it does, reduce the heat to low. Cook uncovered for five minutes. Cover it tightly, and cook for 40 minutes. Don't remove the cover and peek. Go on blind faith. After 40 minutes, remove from heat and set for 10 minutes—without removing the cover. This precise timing method and browning the onion well will give you a perfect pilaf—fit for any dish, no matter how snobbish or simple.

BROILED SCALLOPS

Broiled scallops. Simplicity plus. First, gather the following ingredients:

- 1 pound scallops
- 4 tablespoons butter
- pinch pepper
- pinch salt
- tiny pinch garlic powder
- 2 tablespoons finely chopped onions
- 1 tablespoon of white wine (optional)

This will feed four people, or two to three gluttons. Only kidding. It is a good meal, easy to overdo. Before you start the recipe, turn the broiler on so it will be good and hot. Then, melt four tablespoons of butter, and add a pinch of pepper, salt, and a tiny pinch of garlic powder. Dribble in the wine, stirring. Add the onions, or, if you really want to get fancy, use two finely chopped tablespoons of chives. This substitute adds color. Either way, stir the butter, imparting the onion flavor. Sauté for two minutes.

Liberally brush half this butter on the bottom of a glass pie plate, or four ramekins. Place the scallops in the dish or ramekins, taking care not to crowd them. Baste the scallops with the remainder of the butter, sprinkle on parsley flakes, and pop under the broiler. Watch carefully. It should take only three minutes. When the scallops are golden and just turning from translucent to opaque, serve. What could be simpler!

MAINE SHRIMP IN SHELL

In our way of thinking, few meals have more romance than fresh shrimp cooked in the shell, and served with melted butter, fresh, crusty loaves of French bread, and a Moselle or Chablis wine. Add fresh fruit and cheese for dessert, and you have found a piece of heaven.

You will need one-and-a-half pounds of fresh shrimp for each person fortunate enough to be invited for the feast. This sounds like a glutton's proportion, but the heads must be removed before cooking. Just snap them off and discard, keeping the segmented bodies, shell and all.

When the shrimp are ready, put an inch or so of salted water in a pot, and bring to a boil. If you are cooking several pounds for a large group, use a poultry roaster over two burners instead of a large pot. This distributes the shrimp more evenly so the ones on bottom do not overcook while the ones on top are still raw. Timing is critical with shrimp. It only takes two to two-and-a-half minutes to cook them once the water begins to boil a second time. Overcooking makes them tough and tasteless instead of sweet, tender, and succulent. We prefer cooking shrimp in the shells, feeling the delicate flavor is retained. This is a difficult argument to reasonably refute.

SHRIMP WITHOUT THE SHELL

If you want to get fancy and serve unshelled shrimp as an appetizer, gather the following ingredients.

water
½ **teaspoon salt**
1 **teaspoon lemon juice or vinegar**

Put one-half inch of water in a pot, add the salt and lemon juice or vinegar, and bring to a boil. Timing is crucial. Practically within seconds. Add the cleaned shrimp and watch carefully. As soon as the liquid begins to bubble, time 60 seconds. By then, the shrimp are done. Near the end, test them every few seconds. Just fish one out and nibble on it. The second it has changed from translucent to opaque, remove the pot, drain at once, and dump the shrimp onto a platter. Taking extra caution like this elevates cooks to legends in their own time, within the family at least—where it counts!

DEEP-FRIED SHRIMP

Deep-fried Maine shrimp take a lot of work, but the compliments will be the reward. First, shell some fresh shrimp. Two cups of clear meat will easily serve three to four people. You be the judge. Next, gather the following ingredients:

    vegetable oil
½ **cup flour**
1 **teaspoon salt**
¼ **teaspoon pepper**
2 **cups raw, shelled shrimp**
2 **eggs, beaten**
1 **cup dry bread crumbs**

In a Dutch oven, pour two inches of vegetable oil, and turn the heat to high. When the oil begins to sizzle, reduce heat to medium. This should give a 380° heat, ideal for deep frying. While the oil heats, put the flour, salt, and pepper into a paper bag, and shake it, mixing the dry ingredients. Add the shrimp and shake again, coating each piece thoroughly. Remove the shrimp and dip into the beaten eggs. Then, coat them with bread crumbs and slip into hot oil. It should take only two to three minutes for the two cups of shrimp to cook. Again, as in all shrimp recipes, keep an eagle eye on them, and do not be afraid to nibble one or two. When golden, serve with French fries, cole slaw, tartar sauce, and cold, cold beer. A good ol' American meal.

FRENCH FRIES

French fries appear such a simple dish; yet, most of them we eat, particularly in restaurants, are soggy and greasy. We have three secrets to superb french fries. First, good fries begin with raw potatoes. Second, we soak them several hours in icy cold water, changing the water two or three times. Third, they are cooked in preheated 375° oil.

First, take one potato for each person, peel, and then french into ⅜ to ¼ inch pieces. We like them slender. After the fries are cut up, place them in a large bowl, fill with cold water, and place in the refrigerator. Plan to replace the water two or three times. Something about this procedure makes a crisp, wonderful french fry.

When ready to cook, have the oil at 375°. Drain the potatoes, pat dry with a towel, and slip into the oil. We use a Dutch oven with two to three inches of oil. A frying pan can be dangerous. Cook for 7–10 minutes, or until the fries are golden on the outside; tender on the inside. Remove the French fries, place in a paper bag quickly, and shake for two or three seconds. Immediately dump onto a serving dish. The results will please.

FRIED SMELTS

Smelts have a sweet, delicate flavor so easily enhanced by simplicity. Clean the smelts by eviscerating and cutting off the heads. Put a frying pan on the stove and heat a ¼-inch of oil to 380°. Next, put a half-cup of flour, ½ teaspoon salt, ¼ teaspoon pepper, and a dash of garlic powder into a paper bag. Shake vigorously, mixing dry ingredients. You may dip the smelts in milk. We don't. We just put them in the bag and shake vigorously, coating them thoroughly. Slip them into the hot fat, cooking them a minute or two to the side, depending on size. We like smelts with nothing but cold beer, and maybe, cole slaw. We are too embarrassed to admit the number of smelts we have polished off in a sitting. They are delicate, delicious, just very fine.

Some fine folks advocate batters, bread crumbs, and the like for smelts. We dislike this approach. Smelts are tiny fish, and batter and what-not make a crust that obscures the fish's true flavor.

Smelt shacks get busy in February as anglers try to catch a mess of smelts. Photo courtesy of Maine Department of Inland Fisheries and Wildlife.

RABBIT OVER NOODLES

Rabbit and hare are plentiful little critters, and as far as we can see, were put on Earth solely to be eaten, both by man and every other predator large enough to tackle one. If we come back in another life, we hope it is not as a bunnie.

They are plentiful enough so those simple dishes of January may have become monotonous. An exotic change is in order, and this is one answer. Gather the following:

- 2–3 precooked rabbits, boned
- 4 tablespoons clarified butter, or oil
- 1 large, coarsely chopped onion
- 1 pound chopped mushrooms (fresh)
- 1 teaspoon salt
- ¼ teaspoon pepper
- ¼ teaspoon thyme (optional)
- pinch of garlic powder
- 2 tablespoons flour
- 1 cup water
- 2 cups sour cream

First, simmer the unboned rabbits for two or so hours to tenderize them. Bone completely, and put aside. Over a medium heat, melt the butter or heat the oil. When it begins to sizzle, add chopped onion and mushrooms. Canned mushrooms will work, but fresh are ideal. Put heat on low, and sauté for 30-40 minutes. You can do this quicker, but we like to go slowly with fresh mushrooms. It enhances their delicacy.

When onions and mushrooms are lightly tanned, add the precooked rabbit. When the meat has heated through, push it to the side of the pan, and sprinkle two tablespoons of flour evenly into the pan's bottom. When it begins to brown, remove from heat, and add water slowly, constantly stirring with a whip. Add salt, pepper, thyme, and garlic powder, stirring until gravy thickens. Now, add the two cups of sour cream. Simmer until it thickens to desired consistency for you, then serve on hot, buttered egg noodles. Serve with asparagus and a good Bordeaux wine. A meal fit for royalty, prepared from the lowly bunnie.

HASENPFEFFER

This is similar to Jugged Hare, except for two major differences. It is marinated and made with sour cream. It is sinfully rich. First, gather the following:

- 2-3 rabbits, cut in serving pieces
- 2 cups cider vinegar
- 1 cup dry red wine
- 1 cup water
- 1 tablespoon salt
- 1 teaspoon black pepper
- 1 bay leaf
- 6 whole cloves
- 1 teaspoon dry mustard
- 2 onions, quartered
- 3 tablespoons flour
- 1 tablespoon sugar
- 1 cup sour cream

Cut the two or three rabbits into serving pieces, and place in an earthenware bowl. Cover with the marinade made with the two cups vinegar, one cup of red wine, one cup of water, one tablespoon salt, one teaspoon black pepper, one bay leaf, six whole cloves, one teaspoon dry mustard, and two quartered onions. Mix thoroughly, then place bowl in the refrigerator for 24-48 hours. Turn the pieces occasionally... whenever you think of it.

When ready to cook, remove the pieces from the marinade, wipe dry, then dredge with flour. In a Dutch oven, heat ¼-inch of clarified butter or oil until it sizzles, then place the pieces in without crowding one another. Brown both sides...about five minutes to a side. This initial browning may have to be done in steps if you are unable to get all the pieces in at once. After browning, reduce heat to low, and add enough strained marinade to cover the pieces. After it begins to bubble, cook for 40 minutes. Next, add a tablespoon of sugar. Then, take a paste made with three tablespoons of flour and enough water to make it smooth and somewhat runny, and dribble it into the marinade. Stir with a whip until it thickens. When the desired thickness has been reached, add a cup of sour cream. When it begins to bubble, it is ready to serve. Hasenpfeffer goes well with French bread, a green vegetable such as asparagus, broccoli, or Brussels sprouts, and a good red wine.

BAKED STUFFED HALIBUT

This recipe seems so festive. Fancy restaurants serve it with fancy prices, but it is really simplicity in itself. First, make the *Gourmet Seafood Stuffing* in the June chapter.

Next, lay the pieces of halibut into a shallow baking dish, or better yet, lay each serving piece into a ramekin. Have the bottom of the dish covered with melted butter. Lots of butter makes the dish nice and rich. Place the halibut into a preheated 350° oven, and bake for one-half hour, basting occasionally with butter. Remove from oven, and put stuffing on each piece. We like lots of stuffing. If you have several pieces of fish, you may want to double or triple the stuffing recipe. Sprinkle grated cheese on the stuffing. Parmesan is the thing, but Swiss works just fine. Bake for an additional half hour at 350°. Occasionally baste the stuffing with butter so it will not dry out. Serve with rice pilaf, broccoli, French bread, and your favorite wine.

Winter is upon us, and spring will be a long time coming. We do not mind too much. We dislike rushing time. It goes quickly enough. Even in winter. And February has moments. Many of them memorable.

Chapter 4
March

March. A month of crystalline snow, late winter storms, and half-spring days when the temperature may hit 50°. For some of us, it is a lazy month. Little going on, so we need not feel guilty about hanging around the house. Spring is around the corner, and we'll be busy enough then. For a lot of folks though, this is a busy month. Swollen rivers beckon white-water canoeist weekend after weekend. You have to do it then. The spring run-off won't last. For others, March is the time for cutting next year's wood. That was the custom in pod auger days and it has carried through the ages. One way or the other, spring fever has hit a feverish pitch, and most of us get out, even if it is just for a little while.

Hearty meals, particularly big breakfasts, make this a fine month for cooking. Usually, there are a few packages of venison left, and we know from experience, they are cuts slightly more tender than a hoof. That is why they are still there. Just sitting. Waiting to challenge our culinary skills. But what we really like this month are cooking big breakfasts, leisure affairs that take the better part of the early morning hours. Let's face it. The early morning is always cold. It will only get warmer as the day progresses. Why rush?

Breakfast dishes seem simple. Anyone and their brother can scramble eggs or fry diced, boiled potatoes! However, what appears simple often isn't. With breakfast dishes, crucial timing and exact temperatures make a huge difference in the finished product. Those who master these variables become legends in their time, at least in their family, where it counts.

OMELETTE

You can't ruin an omelette! The worst you may wind up with is a poorly cooked scrambled egg. The secret to a successful omelette is a well-seasoned pan—one that will not stick. Armed with that, half the battle is yours. Next, gather the following ingredients:

    2 **eggs per omelette**
    1 **tablespoon water, milk, or cream**
      pinch of salt
      pinch of black pepper
      tiny pinch garlic powder
    1 **heaping teaspoon parsley (preferably fresh)**
      your choice of filling (cheese, mushrooms,
         or chopped partridge, duck, venison, etc.)
    1 **tablespoon of butter per omelette**

We have an omelette pan made in France. Very nice. Yet, we seem to prefer a cast-iron frying pan, a square one at that! Whatever your choice of utensil, melt a tablespoon of butter over a medium heat. While that gets ready, break two eggs into a bowl. It goes without saying that fresh eggs, really fresh, straight from a local farmer, make superior omelettes. The eggs should be at room temperature, but that is not crucial. Add a tablespoon of liquid. Anyone who knows anything about omelettes knows water is best. Why do we like cream instead? Water makes it lighter and fluffier, but cream imparts a better flavor. Richer. Just a personal preference. Sprinkle in salt, pepper, and about five granules of garlic powder. Beat lightly with a fork.

As soon as the butter sizzles, lift the pan and tilt it back and forth, coating the pan's bottom. Place back on the heat. As soon as it sizzles again, pour in the two, lightly beaten eggs. One secret to a superior omelette is to keep the egg mixture moving. Briskly stir the eggs with a wooden spoon, shaking the pan with the other hand. It should take no more than 60 seconds to do the entire omelette. If it takes longer parts of the egg will overcook, making it tough. To avoid this, remember to keep the butter at that fine line between sizzling hot and high; yet, not so hot the butter browns. Browned butter is the scourge of a good omelette.

As soon as the cooked egg coats the pan's bottom, lift edges and let runny part of egg run underneath. Then, sprinkle in the parsley and filling. Cheese is such a traditional filling, but be adventuresome. Chopped breast of partridge, duck, even venison makes a great filling. Fold the omelette in half. As soon as the runny egg in the center sets, serve. If you are making omelettes for a number of guests, put each aside on a warmed platter in a 200° oven. Not ideal. But the best possible approach.

In the evenings, omelettes go superbly with French fries, French bread and a dry white wine. So continental. And easy. In the morning, serve it with anything traditional. An omelette is a man-sized breakfast.

SHIRRED EGGS AND HAM

This dish looks so festive. An epicurean delight. Yet, it is simpler to make than well-made scrambled egg. The first time we ever had this dish was in a small, isolated valley in Switzerland. It was on the supper menu and we ate it three or four nights in a row. It was that good! First, gather the following ingredients:

3 tablespoons butter
2 eggs per person
   slices of ham...enough
      to cover the bottom
      of pie plate
   salt and pepper

Preheat the oven to 350°. Smear three tablespoons of soft butter on the bottom of a glass pie plate or shallow casserole dish. Lay the slices of ham in, crowding them together tightly. We like the ham to be about a ¼-inch thick. Pop this into the preheated oven and cook for 10–15 minutes, or until the ham and butter really begin to sizzle.

While this cooks, break the eggs into a bowl. When the ham is ready, remove quickly from the oven, dump the eggs on, and put it back into the oven. If the ham is not preheated, the eggs will not cook properly. Naturally, the quicker you put the eggs on and the dish back into the oven, the better the results. Cook for approximately 15 minutes, or until the white solidifies, and the yolk is still runny. Serve immediately. The ham imparts a wonderful flavor to the eggs. Just before serving, you may want to baste the eggs with the butter in the bottom of the dish, then wait for the compliments. Home-made English muffins are excellent with this feast.

SCRAMBLED EGGS

Scrambled eggs should be cooked in a cast-iron frying pan over a low heat. For each serving, break two eggs into a bowl, and add a tablespoon of liquid. Water, milk, or cream are the choices. Put in a pinch of salt, pepper, and a tiny pinch of garlic powder. Beat with a fork, mixing the yolk and white well, but not so much that a froth forms.

Melt two tablespoons of butter in the pan, coat the bottom, and wait for it to bubble. Add the eggs immediately. As the egg mixture firms on the bottom and edges, pull it to the center, leaving the edges runny. The finished product should be loose, creamy, and not the least bit overcooked.

BOILED EGGS

Never boil an egg! It only makes them tough. Instead, heat the water until it is just below the boiling point. Have a teaspoon of salt, a teaspoon of vinegar, and the eggs in the water before it is placed on low heat. These precautions help insure that the shells will not crack while cooking. Once the water reaches the maximum temperature, cook two to three minutes for a solf-boiled egg. Ten minutes for a hard-boiled one. If you use the same amount of water and the same heat setting each time, then you can get amazingly consistent results time after time.

If you want hard-boiled eggs for salads, picnics, and what-not, remove from heat after 10 minutes, and pour cold water over them, cooling them quickly. Just turn the faucet on and keep the water running. Overcooked boiled eggs are tough. Properly cooked ones are a noticeable treat.

FRIED EGGS

Fried eggs are cooked in bacon fat or butter over a medium heat. We like to cook fried eggs quickly. Just the opposite of our scrambled egg philosophy. With a properly seasoned frying pan, no egg dish is easier to prepare. The worst you can do is break a yolk....

This still-life is a scene that has changed little in a century. Throughout this book, over and over again, you will see recommendations for using kitchen tools, utensils, and methods rich in tradition. Part of this is aesthetic nostalgia, but the big reason is quality. Space-age materials have yet to improve on many kitchen tools. Photo courtesy of Maine Department of Inland Fisheries and Wildlife.

March is the month for gathering firewood for the next winter. It builds an appetite. Photo courtesy of Maine Department of Inland Fisheries and Wildlife.

MAINE-STYLE HOMEFRIES

So many cooks look for new, exotic recipes, and never perfect old, simple ones such as homefries. People who take the time and pride to perfect simple foods become legends. Homefries do vary. No two cooks make them taste alike. Precooked potatoes, raw potatoes, seasoning, even the degree of heat changes the flavor. Potatoes are bland, and it takes little to alter the flavor...drastically.

Gather the following ingredients:

- **4–5 medium potatoes, cooked**
- **1 large onion, chopped coarsely**
- **4 tablespoons oil**
- **salt and pepper to taste**
- **pinch of garlic powder**

Some cooks prefer homefries made with potatoes boiled in jackets. We do. Potatoes are less bland this way. Peel and chop into inch cubes. In a frying pan over a medium heat, sauté the onion with garlic powder until the onion turns brown. Putting the garlic in this initial step flavors the oil lightly. Add the potatoes, salt, and pepper, and for an interesting touch if you feel adventuresome, a half teaspoon of poultry seasoning. Brown the potatoes. During this step, don't stir the potatoes a lot. This makes them seem greasier. Why, we don't know. If you brown one side well, turn them and brown some more, then turn a third time and serve as soon as they have browned on that side, the results are great homefries. During the cooking, you may want to add paprika for coloring. We don't.

COOPERS MILLS-STYLE HOMEFRIES

Use the above recipe, but instead of boiled potatoes, use baked potatoes. If you have baked potatoes for supper, throw in four or five extra for the morning homefries. The baked potatoes retain that baked flavor, even after frying. This dish may start a new family tradition.

MASSACHUSETTS-STYLE HOMEFRIES

This is an excellent recipe for the mornings there are no cooked potatoes in the refrigerator. Gather the following:

- 4–5 raw potatoes
- 4 tablespoons oil
- 1 large onion, chopped coarsely
- salt and pepper to taste
- ¼ teaspoon garlic powder
- ½ teaspoon poultry seasoning (optional)
- paprika for color

Peel the potatoes and dice into half-inch cubes. While this operation is going on, have a Dutch oven on a medium heat, sautéing the onion. We like to put the garlic powder in with the onion. When the onion begins to brown, throw in the potatoes, cover, and cook for 15 minutes. Don't even look at it. This steams the potatoes well, making them tender. At the end of 15 minutes, remove the cover, and cook for 8–10 minutes without stirring the potatoes. Then, with a spatula, turn the potatoes over and cook an additional 4–5 minutes. By then, the dish should be ready. If not, cook awhile longer. Don't stir this. It only makes the potatoes greasy. Serve with scrambled eggs, and if you are lucky, maybe a piece of venison tenderloin saved from November. We don't remember why, but this method of cooking homefries reminds us of breakfasts with scrambled eggs, tender venison cuts, and toast made with the previous night's left-over biscuits.

SOUTHERN-STYLE HOMEFRIES

As children, we could make a meal of this dish. All we needed was ketchup, and plenty of it. All you need is one potato per person and a ¼-inch of oil preheated to 380°. Just put the frying pan, or better yet, it is safer, a Dutch oven on a high heat. Pour in the oil and wait for it to sizzle and smoke. Reduce heat to medium, and add potatoes, presliced to ³⁄₁₆-inch thickness. Brown on one side, flip over, and brown on the other. When ready to serve, remove the slices from the oil, quickly put them in a paper bag, quickly shake them, removing excessive grease, and dump onto warmed platter. Lightly salt, and serve with eggs and ham or bacon. Kids love this dish....

WESTERN-STYLE HOMEFRIES

West of the Mississippi, this dish is common fare on breakfast menus. In the northeast, it is unheard of. Gather the following ingredients:

    1 large chopped onion
4–5 raw potatoes
    4 tablespoons oil
       pinch of garlic powder
       salt and pepper to taste
       poultry seasoning (optional)
       paprika for coloring

Grate the potatoes with a cheese grater, making long, thin strings. Have a frying pan sizzling with an ⅛-inch of oil. Add onion, chopped. When it begins to brown, reduce heat to medium-low, and add potatoes. Season with salt, pepper, garlic powder, and paprika. Poultry seasoning is optional, but if you feel adventuresome, add a half teaspoon. It will make folks say, "Geez, what did you do to these homefries?" It could start a family tradition.

Cook the potatoes for 15 minutes. With this recipe, as with all homefry recipes, do not stir while cooking the potatoes. That makes them greasy. After 15 minutes, turn the potatoes like pancakes, and brown the other side. It is not solid, so may break into pieces. That's all right. Just turn all the pieces and cook 15 minutes more. Serve when the potatoes are tender and well-browned. The browner and crispier, the better.

LAZY MAN'S VENISON POT ROAST

So, there you are, staring at a venison roast lying in the bottom of the freezer. It will be a challenge. You suspect a deer hoof may be more tender. Reluctantly, the challenge is accepted, so out it comes for thawing. Relax. It will be superior. Gather the following:

- 3 tablespoons oil or clarified butter
- one roast (venison, bear, or beef)
- 2 chopped onions
- flour
- 2 cups dry red wine
- 2 beef bouillon cubes
- 1 cup boiling water
- 3 whole cloves
- salt and pepper to taste
- ¼ teaspoon garlic powder
- 1 cup sliced, raw carrots
- 5 ounce jar of horseradish (optional)

In an oven-proof Dutch oven over a medium heat, put three tablespoons of oil, or preferably, clarified butter. Add the chopped onions. While they are browning, heavily flour the roast. When the onions begin to brown, add the floured roast. Sear on all sides. When it is good and brown, there will be flour on the pan's bottom. This will be brown and crusty. Turn the heat to high and dump in two cups of wine. Begin scraping the bottom. Keep scraping until it has been somewhat cleaned of flour. Add a cup of boiling water with two dissolved bouillon cubes, three cloves, salt (go lightly because of the bouillon cubes), pepper, garlic powder, and a cup of raw carrots.

Now, if you feel adventuresome, add a five-ounce jar of horseradish. This is a spicy touch, steeped with tradition. If you try it once, it is bound to be a family favorite. When the broth begins to boil again, remove from heat, cover tightly, and put in a preheated 300° oven for three hours, or, are you ready for this, a 200° oven for eight hours! While you spend the day cutting next year's wood, a big, hearty dinner is cooking.

Serve this meal with egg noodles (a delightfully festive touch), French bread, and a green veggie. Biscuits will do nicely, but the wine sauce thickened slightly from the flour on the roast seems to call for the long, slender loaves.

BEER VENISON POT ROAST CANADIAN-STYLE

This is a fine recipe that calls for a bottle of dark beer, but a light lager will do. Gather the following ingredients:

- 2 tablespoons oil
- 1 bay leaf
- a large roast, cubed into stew meat
- 1 huge onion, chopped
- 2 tablespoons flour
- 1 bottle of beer
- ½ cup beef stock
- ½ pound sliced carrots, raw
- 1 tablespoon parsley (preferably fresh)
- salt and pepper to taste
- 2 whole cloves
- 5 ounce jar horseradish (optional)

In an oven-proof Dutch oven, heat oil to moderately high, then throw in a bay leaf. Cook for two minutes. Add the cubed venison, browning quickly on all sides. Add the onions to the venison. When browned, remove from heat and sprinkle in the flour. Put back on stove and lightly brown the flour. When it begins to crust on the pan's bottom, add the beer. Scrape the flour off with a wooden spoon. When it has all been scraped off the bottom, add beef stock (bouillon cube substitute is all right), parsley, salt, pepper, and cloves and cover tightly. Bring to a boil, then place in a preheated 275° oven for 2½ hours. Stir occasionally and add more liquid when needed. The liquid may be beer.

This meal is better reheated once it has been initially cooked. Either way, add the carrots about one hour before serving time. When they become tender, the meal is ready. If you are going to be adventuresome and use horseradish, add this as soon as you put the Dutch oven into the oven.

If you do not have an oven-proof Dutch oven, try putting aluminum foil on the handles that may be affected by heat. This should protect them.

Serve this meal with buttered egg noodles, French bread, and a green veggie. In March, asparagus, spinach, and celery are plentiful in the supermarkets. This time of year, these three vegetables are at their finest. Enjoy.

DEER BURGER

Deer burger is another frozen food that seems to get by-passed in the freezer month after month. It makes excellent meat balls with spaghetti, particularly when it is mixed with pork sausage.

One easy, quick way to prepare a fine meal from deer burger is to begin with a frozen hunk of burger! On a medium heat, bring oil, or preferably, clarified butter, to a sizzle. Throw in two large, chopped onions. As they begin to turn translucent, push them aside and add two tablespoons of flour. Throw the hunk of deer burger beside it, and let it begin to cook. The onions will get browner, and the flour will begin to crust and get brown. About this time, that inevitable water in the frozen meat begins to melt and cover the pan's bottom. Begin scraping the flour off the bottom. This will make a delightful gravy. Add a ¼-teaspoon of garlic powder, salt and pepper to taste, and continue cooking the deer burger. The second this deer burger has all turned from pink to brown, serve immediately with biscuits, buttered-parsleyed potatoes, and string beans.

Once, we cooked this on Chamberlain Lake after a long day of driving and then canoeing. One fellow claimed he disliked deer meat of any kind. Hunger overcame him in the end, and he tried this simple dish. Two helpings later, he allowed deer meat was really not half bad.

It can be a lazy or busy time of year. Eat, drink, and smile a lot. Spring with its glories is but a moment away.

Chapter 5
April

April showers bring May flowers. But first, what about all this white stuff? In our part of the country, this month seldom delivers its true promise of spring. Late winter storms and thigh-deep snow, particularly around black growth on the north side of ridges, make April sometimes feel like February.

A few of us manage to catch some trout this month, adverse weather conditions or not. Along toward the end of April when the leaves on the alders get as big as a mouse's ear, and the black flies become intolerable, we often catch lots of trout! Many are released for another day, but a few become the main course in the year's finest meals.

Trout. How we love them! And, when we say trout, we mean brook trout—that gourmet delight in the char family. However, for any of these recipes, brown trout or rainbow trout are excellent substitutes. We have never turned down a helping of them. We also know trout means brown trout in Europe, and those folks know something about preparing trout dishes. You might say they pioneered the rules on trout cookery.

This month has other offerings from the wilds. As soon as lawns and fields become bare of snow for a short time, dandelion greens appear. With a butter knife and shallow, rectangular basket, it takes no time to get a mess of them. Some folks pile these greens in a pail, getting the bottom ones dirty from the roots of the top ones. This makes cleaning them nearly impossible. We have the soiled part of the greens together, making the cleaning job easy. The basket makes them easy to pile in this manner.

Dandelion greens are best immediately after they poke through the ground. A few days later, they are tough and, worse yet, bitter. This is probably the single largest reason folks turn their noses up at this easily obtainable food so high in vitamins A and C. They have eaten a batch of greens picked after they have matured too much. When picked young, dandelion greens are a delight.

One real gourmet delight, fiddleheads, appears near the end of this month. The young ostrich fern is an epicurean delight that goes with trout like peaches go with cream. It grows in rich, damp soil along streams and rivers, and is impossible to confuse with bracken fern. Ostrich fern has a pronounced groove on the inside of the stem; bracken fern does not. It is that simple.

SAUTÉED TROUT

This is our favorite method of preparing trout. Simplicity in itself. Melt three tablespoons of butter in a cast-iron frying pan over a medium-low heat. It is a good idea to clarify the butter so it will not burn as quickly as plain butter. Next, put in a pinch of garlic powder, lightly flavoring the butter. It must only be a pinch. Trout has a delicate flavor easily overpowered. Put a half-cup of flour, a dash of pepper, and a touch of salt in a paper bag. Shake the bag, mixing the ingredients well. Throw in the cleaned trout, then shake vigorously, coating them with flour. Remove them, and lightly brush the cavities with butter from the frying pan. Place the trout in the frying pan. It should be just hot enough so there is a little sizzle when the cold trout touches the pan's bottom. A large trout may have to be cooked four or so minutes per side. For a small one, only one to two minutes per side will do. As soon as the meat along the backbone turns from translucent to opaque, remove quickly, and serve with fiddleheads, buttered-parsleyed potatoes, French bread, and a good Chablis. Splurge. This is one of the finest meals this country has to offer.

MAINE-STYLE TROUT

This recipe makes gourmets shudder. As children, this seems to be the only way we remember trout meals served. In a cast-iron frying pan over a medium heat, bacon fat was brought to a smoking sizzle. The trout were rolled in cornmeal and slipped into the pan. Later, cooked to a snapping crispness, they were served, often with eggs and bacon. This method breaks all fish cookery rules. The fish is over-done, the bacon fat is overpowering, and the cornmeal has absorbed grease. However, a lot of fine folks eat trout year after year prepared in this manner. We do sometimes. Just for nostalgic reasons, of course, or so we try to tell ourselves.

OVEN-FRIED TROUT

A superior recipe. And, so simple. Put a half-stick of butter in a shallow baking dish, and place in a preheated 500° oven for five minutes. In the meantime, beat an egg and three tablespoons of milk. Stir in a half teaspoon of paprika for color. Dip the trout in this mixture and roll in dried bread crumbs, coating liberally. Lay the trout in the hot baking dish, and pop back into the oven. Bake for eight minutes, or until the trout are done. Serve with a superior French Chablis, French bread, buttered-parsleyed potatoes, and frenched string beans with slivered almonds.

SPITTED TROUT

Spitted trout brings back fond memories of childhood. With a couple of friends, we caught trout from a large woodland pool. We caught them with great regularity. We had a fire going, made with dry maple and beech, and as soon as each one of us caught a trout, we would clean it immediately, skewer it with a green alder stick, and place it over red-hot coals. What an epicurean delight. Maybe the setting. Maybe the friends. But with the smoky flavor imparted from the maple and beech coals, seasoning was unnecessary, and we have never enjoyed trout more.

GRILLED TROUT

Another recipe for the outdoors. Simplicity in itself. Grilled is a fine way to prepare trout, particularly when the fish are 12–15 inches long. After cleaning the fish, place five inches above medium-dark hardwood coals. Baste lightly with melted butter that has been seasoned lightly with a pinch of garlic powder. Cook four to seven minutes per side, depending on the size of the trout. Try not to overcook. As soon as the meat along the backbone turns from translucent to opaque, the trout are ready. Remember, the idea in fish cookery is to coagulate the body juices, not tenderize the flesh, so never overcook. Keep a watchful eye and serve trout that is moist and succulent instead of dry and tasteless. You'll be a legend.

TROUT CHOWDER

Trout chowder! Who ever heard of trout chowder! Well, we have. Once, with the West Branch of the Penobscot and Katahdin in the background, we ate three bowls of trout chowder with plenty of hot cups of tea and home-made biscuits. A rare treat. Try making trout chowder. The recipe for fish chowder is back in Chapter 2. You shall not regret it.

POACHED TROUT

Poaching is one of the best ways to cook a delicately flavored fish such as trout. This method helps retain the delicate taste so easily lost with harsher heats. First, gather the following ingredients:

- **6 cups water**
- **¼ cup vinegar**
- **1 onion, quartered**
- **1 stalk celery, quartered**
- **1 teaspoon salt**
- **2 cloves**
- **1 cup dry white wine (optional)**

Bring this mixture to a smiling bubble, and cook for 10 minutes. Keep this mixture on a low heat. Poaching means to poach—not boil. Take the cleaned trout, and slip them into the bouillon. Don't put in so many it crowds them. When the water begins to bubble again, cook six to 10 minutes, depending on the size of the fish. Keep a careful eye. When the meat along the backbone first turns from translucent to opaque, serve with buttered-parsleyed potatoes and a mild green vegetable. A good white wine and French bread will round out a meal heavenly already.

TRUITES À LA MEUNIÈRE

A classic French recipe...simple and elegant and rich. Over a medium heat, place an iron frying pan with a ¼-inch of oil, preferably peanut oil. This is not crucial. While the oil heats, dry cleaned trout with a paper towel, dip in milk, then dredge in flour seasoned with salt, pepper, and a pinch of garlic powder. Brown the fish on both sides, and remove as soon as the flesh along the backbone turns from translucent to opaque; yet, is still moist. Lay the fish on a warmed serving platter. Garnish the fish lightly with lemon juice, then parsley and black pepper. Quickly pour the oil from the pan, put in one tablespoon of butter for each serving, and cook until the butter turns a rich brown. Gently pour this butter over the trout, and serve with a Graves white wine, rice pilaf, broccoli, and French bread. Like so many French dishes, it is elegant, easy to prepare, and particularly enhances any food gathered in the wilds....

An early season brook trout . . . the making of a fine meal.   Photo courtesy of Maine Department of Inland Fisheries and Wildlife.

BAKED LAKE TROUT
"Togue"

Lake trout particularly lend themselves to baking, preferably on a wire rack so fish will not lie in the somewhat oily juices while cooking. First, take a lake trout, clean it, and rub inside and out with a mixture made from one-to-two teaspoons salt and the juice of two lemons. Really scour the fish with this. Then, gather the following ingredients:

> 2 cups dry bread crumbs
> small can mushrooms, juice and all
> 4 tablespoons melted butter
> 1 large, coarsely chopped onion
> 1 stalk celery, finely chopped
> 1 teaspoon poultry seasoning
> salt and pepper to taste
> enough milk or cream to moisten stuffing

Over a medium-low heat, sauté the onion, celery, and mushrooms in four tablespoons of butter. Make sure to save the juice from the can of mushrooms to add later. When the onion first turns translucent, remove from heat and dump the onions, celery, mushrooms, and melted butter into a bowl with the dry bread crumbs, mushroom juice, poultry seasoning, salt, pepper, and enough milk or cream to make a moist stuffing. This stuffing should be enough to loosely fill the cavity of a four-to-five pound trout. Secure the cavity with roasting pins. You may double, triple, and so forth the recipe to accommodate larger fish for luckier anglers.

Lay a wire rack on a shallow baking dish, lay the fish on the rack, baste heavily with butter, and put into a preheated 350° oven. The fish's size will determine cooking time. A four-to-five-pound fish should cook in 40-50 minutes. Keep a careful eye on it near the end, occasionally flaking a tiny piece away from the backbone. When it turns from translucent to opaque; yet, still moist and succulent, serve with mashed potatoes, peas, rye bread, and Bordeaux wine.

This is a fine meal, particularly when you take the pains to baste it with fresh, melted butter instead of the somewhat oily butter under the fish. This is one of those small things that impress discriminating palates, raising some cooks to legends in their circle of friends.

WILDERNESS LAKE TROUT

A superior recipe for grilling lake trout over coals. It will impress friends in two ways. First, it is an epicurean delight! Second, you need fresh mint, an easy plant to identify, that seems to grow in abundance anywhere there are forests, pristine lakes, and hungry lake trout.

"Wild Mint"

First, gather some mint. Usually an easy task. It grows on water edges in dark green clumps. Mint has lance-shaped leaves, and it is impossible to confuse with anything else. Its aromatic scent is a sure sign, but this plant has another identifying characteristic. The stem is four sided instead of round. When you find a good patch, pick a bunch, dry, and save for tea as well as backyard Wilderness Lake Trout. It will keep for years. Our kitchen always has jars of this wonderful herb.

Gather the following ingredients:

- 1 four-to-five-pound fish
- ¼ cup oil
- juice from two fresh lemons
- 4 heaping teaspoons chopped mint leaves
- salt and pepper to taste
- ½ teaspoon thyme (optional)
- 1 teaspoon dill weed (optional)

Over a low heat, combine the oil, preferably olive, lemon juice, mint leaves, salt, pepper, and optional herbs, and cook for 10-15 minutes, stirring occasionally.

Put a well-oiled grill four-to-five inches above medium-dark coals, brush the fish with the mint-oil mixture, and lay on grill. Brush several times with this mixture during the cooking. When the fish is golden and flaky, serve with mashed potatoes, a green vegetable, and if you want to make a wilderness setting really elegant, a good white wine. Yet, it seems we have always had beer with this dish, and loved every bottle of it. Maybe it is the mint. Maybe the setting where we have eaten this delight. Beer seemed to work well.

BLUE TROUT

This elegant recipe has its roots in Europe. It is a real gourmet recipe few people have ever tried; yet, it is basically simple. The only problem is the need for live trout, but remember those days on a favorite stream when you were unable to go wrong. Merely carry a pail or small cooler to your favorite pool, and drop the trout in it. If there is ice in the container, all the better.

When you have enough for a meal, either head home or cook them on the bank with a fire or Coleman stove. No method enhances the delicate flavor of trout more than this one. Truly. Get a solution boiling made from a quart of water, one-and-a-half cups of vinegar, 1 teaspoon salt, and a few peppercorns. Peppercorns are optional. The vinegar and water measurements should be exact. The finished product will literally be blue—a combination of the trout's natural body film and the acidic solution for cooking.

After the water begins boiling, hit each trout on the head, killing them, then eviscerate quickly, handling them as little as possible. Try not to remove too much of the natural film on the fish. Plunge a couple of fish at a time into the solution. When the solution begins to gently bubble again, reduce the heat and simmer for six to 10 minutes. Again, like all trout recipes, watch it carefully. As soon as the meat along the backbone turns opaque, remove and serve. If this meal is prepared on a trout stream, French bread and a superior Chablis, and plenty of it, are all anyone needs to feel like royalty.

FIDDLEHEADS

Fiddleheads are a prized delicacy that particularly lend themselves to steaming. You may steam them, or cook them in an inch of water with a ½-teaspoon of salt. Whatever way you choose, get the water boiling, then add the young ostrich ferns, picked when they were between two-to-five-inches tall. Cook until tender. This should take seven to eight minutes after the water has begun to bubble a second time. Be careful not to overcook fiddleheads. This is a general rule of thumb with so many veggies, but of particular importance to this delicate fern. Overcooking makes them slimy. Very unappetizing. A poor way to treat this spring delicacy. Serve fiddleheads lightly seasoned with salt and pepper, and a dollop of butter. This vegetable goes superbly with trout, buttered-parsleyed potatoes, French bread, and a superior bottle of dry white wine. Paradise enough.

Once, we had fiddleheads with hollandaise sauce, and were more than impressed. You might want to try this combination. After you have eaten two or three of the season's first messes of fiddleheads, hollandaise sauce is a good change of pace.

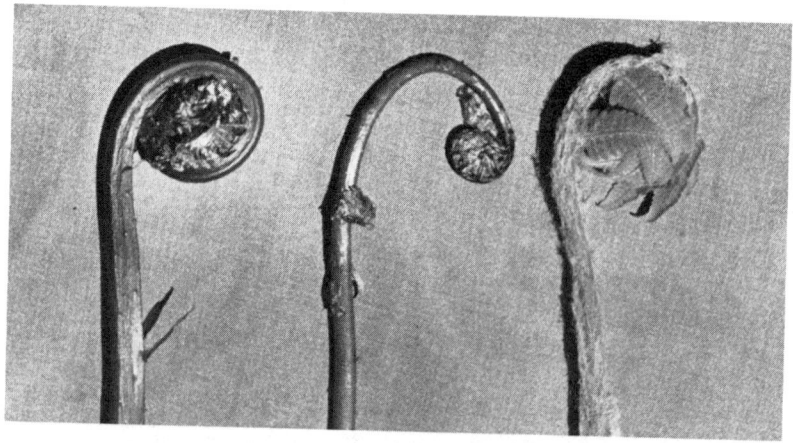

Fiddleheads fern on left. Others are ferns but not edible.

"Recognizing Fiddleheads"

Fiddleheads are young *ostrich ferns*. They grow in clumps along rich, fertile banks, and are easy to identify. There is a very pronounced groove on the inside of the stem. Bracken fern, a plant commonly mistaken for the edible fern, has little or no groove at all. Once you have identified ostrich fern, you can identify it from incredible distances, simply by its distinguished shade of green.

DANDELION GREENS

These tiny shoots come so early in the spring everything around them is brown. Backwoods dandelion greens connoisseurs swear greens picked in fields as opposed to lawns are superior. Whatever place you choose, use a butter knife and shallow rectangular basket, and pick them when they just poke through the ground. If you wait until later, and pick mature ones, they are tough, and worse yet, bitter. We like shallow baskets for gathering greens instead of pails. With the latter, we tend to lay the dirty bottoms of the plants on top of one another. With the basket, the bottom parts are all in line. It makes them much easier to clean. Remember, soil this time of year tends to be very damp, sticking on everything. Gritty greens are unappetizing.

We merely take an inch of salted butter, and boil and steam these tender leaves for five to seven minutes over a medium-low heat. We serve them with cider vinegar and huge dollops of butter. Buttered potatoes, buttermilk biscuits, fried white perch, and steaming cups of coffee make dandelion greens memorable.

Some recipes advocate boiling the greens once for two or three minutes, pouring off the water, and adding new water seasoned with salt. The idea is the greens are too bitter unless this procedure is followed. For older, maturer greens, this may be a necessity. We always pick them young, and do not have this problem.

Other recipes call for long cooking times, an hour or more, with pieces of lean salt pork. This is an ancient, time-honored method. We remember these meals from childhood well.

MAINE-STYLE DANDELION GREENS

This meal will take two to three hours, and was traditionally an entire meal in itself. First, gather the following ingredients:

> **enough greens to fill Dutch oven**
> 1 **pound lean salt pork**
> **salt and pepper to taste**
> ½ **teaspoon dry mustard**
> **small, chunked potatoes**

In a Dutch oven, lay a piece of salt pork that has been cut into five or six pieces. Add a half teaspoon of dry mustard, and then cover the pork slightly with water. On a medium heat, bring it to a smiling boil, reduce the heat, and let simmer for 1½ to 2 hours. You may have to add water occasionally. At the end of this initial cooking time, add the dandelion greens, season, cover, and cook for an hour. Stir occasionally. A half-hour before serving time, bury the potatoes in the greens, and cover again. The amount of potatoes depends on the number of people being served. When the potatoes are done, serve with lots of butter, vinegar, and coffee or tea. It is a greasy dish, yet, so flavorful because of the slow simmering.

BRAISED WOODCHUCK

So many people associate this animal with July. During that month, woodchucks raise havoc with snapped beans in the garden, and the haying season is in full swing, leaving these poor little critters standing in the middle of open fields, really exposed.

We associate this animal with July also, but prefer eating one in April a few weeks after they have fed on tender new shoots, fattening them from winter. We are unopposed to eating any woodchuck harvested during the summer, but those inevitable bug bites sometimes are difficult to contend with and are very unappetizing. In April, there are few bug bites, if any, and we feel we are getting a head start on saving the garden.

Woodchucks are certainly worth eating. After eviscerating and skinning, remove the small glands from the inside of the front leg, cut the body into serving pieces, and soak in a solution of water and a tablespoon of salt for a few hours. You might want to change the water a couple of times until all the blood is removed.

When ready to cook, gather the following ingredients:

- 3 tablespoons oil
- 1 woodchuck, cut into serving pieces
- 2 chopped onions
- 2 tablespoons flour
- 2 cups dry red wine
- 1 cup boiling water
- 2 beef bouillon cubes
- 6 cloves
- salt and pepper to taste
- 1 cup sliced carrots
- ¼ teaspoon garlic powder
- ⅛ teaspoon of both tarragon and basil (optional)

Place a Dutch oven on a medium heat, and add three tablespoons of oil and two onions. When the onions begin to brown, pat the pieces of woodchuck dry with a paper towel, and add to the pot. Sear pieces quickly. If the woodchuck is large, this searing may have to be done in steps. Not all the pieces can be done at once. Set them aside.

Once the pieces have been seared, turn the heat to high and sprinkle in two tablespoons of flour. When it begins to brown and crust in good shape, dump in two cups of dry red wine. There should be a hissing roar and a lot of the flour will lift from the pan's bottom. Begin scraping the rest off with a wooden spoon. Stir constantly, breaking up any lumps. Dissolve two bouillon cubes in a cup of boiling water, and add that, six cloves, salt, pepper, cup of sliced, raw carrots, quarter teaspoon of garlic powder, and tarragon and basil. The last two are optional. When it boils again, reduce heat to low and let simmer for three hours.

If you prefer a boneless meal, after the first hour, bone the woodchuck carefully. Return pieces to broth and keep simmering for an additional two hours. Try not to add any additional water. The sauce should be thickened somewhat near the end from the flour, and the wine will make a rich sauce. Serve with egg noodles and a green veggie. Rye bread, and plenty of it, and a good domestic dry red wine will make this meal memorable, even for a reluctant dinner guest.

April usually begins drab and dull, but ends on the upswing, promising us the glories of the green season just moments away.

The rich flesh of a woodchuck makes a memorable meal.   Ken Allen photo.

Chapter 6
May

May. Here it comes. Sunlight and more sunlight. The ice is gone. Finally. The water is blue. The sky bluer. And vivid greens everywhere, bursting across rolling countryside. The wind blows. A lot. Astute observers don't mind though. It dries gardens for early planting, and days are usually warm anyway. The year at its finest. Intoxicating. The essence of paradise.

This is a grand month for outdoorsmen. Hopefully, May Day finds you with the yard cleaned and groomed and next year's wood cut. You have little better to do under the sun than wait for the garden to dry, and go fishing. So often, salmon is the quarry. A lot of fine folks associate salmon with July...Fourth of July and all...but more of these silver leapers land in anglers' nets this month than any other. This month finds us preparing a lot of salmon dishes, one of the world's most delicious and romantic foods.

Another epicurean delight this month is asparagus. If you have an asparagus patch at your house, this food will be coming out of your ears. If you have no patch at home, the chances are good, particularly if you are a bird or deer hunter, you will know about one or two patches around old homesteads. We do, and take good advantage of these finds that have outlasted the folks who planted them.

Fidddleheads will still be in great abundance, particularly along shaded banks and in more northern climes. More exotic recipes are in order. No matter how fine this food may be, you need a change of pace. May is also the time to find morel mushrooms, a real gourmet delight.

So many days afield are the stuff dreams are made of . . . Author searches for Atlantic salmon . . . one of nature's real gourmet delights. Ken Allen photo.

BAKED SALMON

A common complaint about salmon is its dryness. When folks tell us salmon is too dry for their palates, we point out in the most polite manner that dry salmon is the result of overcooking. And, we know how easy it is to overcook salmon. This is an exaggeration, but one second salmon is undercooked; a second later, too well-done. An exaggeration all right. But it illustrates how closely this fish must be watched during cooking. As soon as the flesh along the backbone turns from a translucent pink to a cloudy, moist pink, remove to a serving dish. The results will be moist, succulent chunks of salmon fit for the gods.

A stuffing is nice for a baked salmon. We like a simple Poultry Bread Stuffing. You will need six cups for a 10-pound salmon; two-and-a-half cups for a four-pound fish. Some folks like to sew or pin the body cavity together. So often, we don't bother.

If the idea of a Poultry Bread Stuffing is unappealing, try this mushroom stuffing, particularly for smaller fish. Gather the following ingredients:

Mushroom Stuffing

- 4 tablespoons butter
- ½ cup chopped onions
- ½ cup chopped celery, leaves and all
- 1 cup sliced mushrooms
- ½ cup dry bread crumbs
- 1 teaspoon parsley (preferably fresh)
- pinch of garlic powder
- ¼ teaspoon marjoram (optional)
- ¼ teaspoon dill weed (optional)
- salt and pepper to taste

Over a medium-low heat, melt four tablespoons butter, and then add chopped onions, chopped celery, and sliced mushrooms. Just when the onions begin to tan, remove from heat. Put in a bowl with the dry bread crumbs, parsley, garlic powder, and optional marjoram and dill weed. (Dill weed really goes with fish like peaches with cream.) Mix thoroughly and stuff fish. You may have to double, triple, or even halve this recipe, all dependent on the fish.

Lay the fish on a greased baking sheet, stuff, and brush heavily with a sauce made simply from a stick of butter, and a tablespoon of dry white wine or a tablespoon of fresh lemon juice. Place in a preheated 400° oven for approximately 10 minutes per pound (dressed weight). Baste often during the cooking. Near the end, keep a watchful eye. If you are unsure of yourself, occasionally flake off a tiny piece near the backbone. That is a sure method of perfect salmon.

Serve baked salmon with boiled potatoes drenched with butter lightly seasoned with garlic powder and parsley, frenched string beans and slivered almonds, home-made white bread, and a good bottle of white wine. Enjoy one of the world's finest delights—salmon cooked to perfection.

SAUTÉED SALMON

This recipe is our most common way of preparing salmon, particularly the smaller ones. Simplicity in itself. Cut a cleaned salmon into steaks one-inch thick. Leave the skin on. In a cast-iron frying pan over a medium-low heat, melt two or three tablespoons of butter. You may clarify the butter. We do not bother. The cooking time is short and the heat low. Scorched butter is not a problem. We sprinkle a bit of pepper on the steaks, just a touch, and slip them into the pan. It only takes about four minutes per side, but again, keep an eagle eye on it, and when the flesh next to the bone turns from translucent pink to cloudy pink, lay on a serving plate, drench with butter from the pan, and serve. Mashed potatoes, string beans, home-made white bread, and a good white wine round out this simple meal. Garnish the potatoes with parsley, and pretend you are royalty. It won't be difficult.

BROILED SALMON

One of our most memorable meals of all times was in a wilderness setting close to Rangeley, Maine. We had two salmon in the live-well of a boat. After the campfire had burned down to a good bed of maple coals, we killed the fish, quickly cleaned them, steaked them to one-inch thickness, and put them on a grill six inches from the heat. The coals were a perfect heat. You could hold your hand five seconds six inches from the coals. A good test for proper temperature for grilling fish.

With its somewhat oily flesh, salmon really lends itself to broiling. We cooked these steaks four minutes to a side, keeping a careful eye near the end. We had nothing but broiled salmon, cooked to perfection, and steaming cups of coffee. There was no seasoning, butter, or bread. But it did not matter. We have eaten in restaurants throughout Europe and North America, so many of them memorable delights, but none matched that primitive repast.

Steaking a salmon. Photo courtesy of Maine Department of Inland Fisheries and Wildlife.

PLANKED SALMON

This is nothing more than baked salmon, but the plank adds a festive touch. The entire meal with all the hot side dishes is artfully placed on the plank and delivered to the table.

This dish begins with a hardwood plank. Don't use a laminated cutting board. First, pour boiling water over a plank and let it soak for a half hour. When ready to use, wipe dry, then oil. The soaking keeps the board from bursting into flames, although we have never heard of this happening, even with folks who don't take the precaution. Oil the board well, and lay a small salmon upon it. Three to four pounds is fine. A big Atlantic salmon takes a long cooking time, and the plank really will burst into flames.

Stuff the salmon just as in the baked salmon recipe, brush with a mixture of melted butter (one stick) and a tablespoon of dry white wine, and put in a 400° oven for 10 minutes a pound. When ready, surround the fish with mashed potatoes, winter squash (mashed), and peas with pearl onions. A loaf of French bread and a good bottle of dry white wine make this memorable. The plank adds such a festive touch. Who'd ever believe it?

POACHED SALMON

Poaching is a gentle way to cook fish, enhancing its delicate flavor. In Europe and the Maritime Provinces, poached fish is common. It has never caught on in the U.S. Give it a try. It may start a family tradition.

You may want to get fancy and make a court bouillon. Gather the following ingredients:

- 1 quart water
- ½ cup of white wine
- 1½ teaspoons salt
- 1 onion, quartered
- 2 cloves, stuck in onion pieces
- ½ carrot, quartered
- leafy part of celery stalk
- 4 peppercorns
- 1 bay leaf
- 6 sprigs parsley
- 1 sprig thyme

Put these ingredients together in a Dutch oven and simmer over a low heat for 30 minutes. You may want to strain it before poaching fish. We don't....

As we said, you may want to get fancy and make this *court bouillon*. However, there have been times when we were on the backside of the mountain, really hankering for poached salmon. We have had salmon, but the best we could manage for *court bouillon* was a quart of water, ½-cup of vinegar, salt, onion, carrot, and with luck, maybe a celery stalk. No one felt abused. The salmon was delicately excellent. In short, if you do not have a sprig of thyme or other ingredients, don't abandon the idea of poaching a salmon. The liquid is versatile!

In Canada, poached salmon steaks are a common dish. Similar to broiling or sautéing, the steaks are one-inch thick, and may be poached in the Dutch oven. However, for a whole fish, use a poultry roaster on two burners, and wrap the fish in cheese cloth so it will not fall apart when lifting it from the bouillon.

Bring the liquid to a smiling, gentle bubble. Add the steaks or whole fish. Once it begins to bubble again, begin timing the cooking. With steaks, cook four minutes, then with a spatula, turn them over and cook an additional four minutes. Turning them is not crucial, but they cook more evenly. Why it works that way baffles us. With a whole fish, cook 8–10 minutes per pound. If you are unsure if the fish is done, flake a little flesh from the backbone. When it first turns from translucent pink to cloudy pink, remove immediately.

Serve poached salmon with lemon wedges, lots of melted butter, buttered-parsleyed potatoes, a delicate green vegetable, home-made bread, and a good white wine. One meal of poached fish usually convinces newcomers to this method that they have been missing something. Poached fish of any kind is a memory. Pure and simple.

SALMON LOAF

It sort of embarrasses us to admit this, but salmon loaf is our favorite way to prepare fresh salmon. The first one to land in our net each season winds up in this manner. It is enough to make a self-respecting gourmet shudder, but we love it.

Gather the following ingredients:

- **2 cups clear meat**
- **1 cup dry bread crumbs or crackers**
- **1 cup cream or evaporated milk**
- **1 heaping tablespoon finely chopped onions**
- **1–2 eggs**
- **pepper and salt to taste**

You may use canned salmon for this recipe. As children, we ate a lot of salmon loaf from the canned variety. Just remember, canned foods are salty, so go easy on the salt.

The ideal is fresh salmon. Lay the salmon in a Dutch oven. If it is large enough for two cups of clear meat, it will have to be cut in half. Barely cover the pieces with cold water, throw in a quartered onion, and place on a *low* heat. Simmer until the meat along the backbone turns from translucent pink to cloudy pink; remove from the liquid immediately. When cool, skin and bone completely.

Put the two cups of clear meat in a large bowl, add the bread crumbs or cracker crumbs, cup of cream (my preference) or evaporated milk, finely chopped onion, one or two beaten eggs, and salt and pepper to taste. One egg is frugality, but two make the loaf lighter in texture. A real plus.

Mix ingredients thoroughly, put into a well-buttered bread-loaf pan, dot with chunks of butter, and bake in a 350° preheated oven for 30 minutes, or until it just sets. If it stays longer, it crusts and becomes drier. Serve with scalloped potatoes, peas, home-made white bread, and a Graves white wine. This is not a great wine, but salmon loaf does not have the epicurean appeal of a dish like Coquilles St. Jacques or sautéed trout. But, it is good country cooking food. Just so fine.

SCALLOPED POTATOES

A simple dish. So delightful. Gather the following ingredients:

- 3 onions, peeled and sliced thinly
- 6 potatoes, peeled and sliced thinly
- 2½ cups milk
- 4 tablespoons butter
- 3 tablespoons flour
- 1 teaspoon salt
- ½ teaspoon pepper
- 1 small onion, grated
- paprika

Peel and thinly slice three onions, then peel and thinly slice six potatoes. Now, you are ready to make a white sauce.

Atlantic salmon fishing on the Penobscot River.   Photo courtesy of Maine Department of Inland Fisheries and Wildlife.

White Sauce

In a saucepan over a medium-low heat, melt four tablespoons of butter. Evenly sprinkle in three tablespoons of flour. When the flour begins to bubble, cook for 60 seconds, stirring with a whip. Do not allow the flour to brown. If you suspect it is about to brown, remove immediately from the heat. Once the saucepan has been removed, dribble in two-and-a-half cups of milk, stirring constantly with a whip. When the milk has been added, put in a teaspoon of salt and half a teaspoon of pepper. Put back on the medium-low heat, and continue stirring. When it begins to thicken noticeably, cook for five minutes, and continue stirring. Remove from heat.

In a heavily buttered, deep casserole dish, put a layer of potatoes on the bottom, then a thin layer of the onions. Pour some white sauce over this. Repeat the layers until everything has been added. Grate an onion on top, color with paprika, cover, and place in a 325°oven for 40 minutes, then uncover, and cook an additional 70 minutes. This long cooking time with the low heat keeps the milk from curdling.

ASPARAGUS

You will need one-and-a-half pounds of asparagus for serving four people. To prepare, break off the bottoms of the stalks where they are not tough and snap easily. Clean thoroughly under a gentle stream of water with a vegetable brush. People who have never picked their own asparagus do not understand what a miserable job this can be. When ready, heat an inch of salted water in a coffee pot. That's right! We like to stand this vegetable on its bottom while cooking. Cook for seven to 10 minutes and serve with any elegant main dish.

CREAMED ASPARAGUS

Cook asparagus using the above method. When done, cut the asparagus in inch long pieces, and add them with the cooking water to a saucepan with thickened white sauce. Serve this delight on thick slices of toasted, home-made white bread. A superior change of pace meal for times when the ole' tummy does not feel up to snuff.

CREAMED FIDDLEHEADS

Cook fiddleheads for seven to eight minutes in an inch of lightly salted water. When tender, remove from heat and add these tender greens, juice and all, to a saucepan of thickened white sauce. Serve on thick slices of toasted, home-made white bread. Later, contentedly sit back, and try to decide which meal is best, creamed fiddleheads or creamed asparagus? They are both delightful.

FIDDLEHEAD SALAD

Cook cleaned fiddleheads in one inch of lightly salted water for seven or eight minutes, or until they become tender. When done, mix with an equal amount of a mixture made with raw onions and raw mushrooms. Marinate for at least 12 hours in an Italian dressing, then serve as an appetizer. Simple and delightful.

MORELS

Morels are easy mushrooms to identify. They have conical caps that are tan or brown. The real identifying characteristic is the pits and ridges on the cap, making this part of the mushroom look like brown tripe. Just one word of caution. This mushroom does resemble an odd looking one in the Gyromitra genus that is reputed to be poisonous. The Gyromitra mushroom has a cap resembling a brown "brain" perched on a thick white stick. The cap is not conical nor does it have sharp, pitted ridges like the morel mushroom. They are easy to identify, but be careful.

Pick only the firmest, freshest morels, leaving the brownish, somewhat caved-in ones alone. Some folks advocate never washing mushrooms. Probably good advice. We do not follow it though. Mushrooms, particularly after a rain that splashes dirt on them, tend to be gritty. It is difficult and tedious to pick each particle off, and we have never been clever enough to figure out another method, other than water.

Angler casting into quick water, hoping to catch some trout or salmon for an epicurean delight. Photo courtesy of Maine Department of Inland Fisheries and Wildlife.

SAUTÉING MUSHROOMS

For each half pound of mushrooms, melt two to three tablespoons of butter in a cast-iron frying pan over a low heat. Slice the mushrooms and add them to the pan. Cook until the edges begin to brown. Over a low heat, this may take 30 minutes, depending on the amount of liquid in the mushrooms. Watch the dish occasionally and stir gently with a wooden spoon. Try not to overcook this delicate food. It only makes them black, and worse yet, rubbery. Season lightly with salt and pepper. Don't use anything to overpower the delicate, subtle flavor of the mushroom.

CREAMED MUSHROOMS ON TOAST

A great recipe for times when you feel like a light meal instead of a feast. Also, it makes a fine appetizer. Gather the following ingredients:

- 1 pound mushrooms
- 4–5 tablespoons butter
- 3 tablespoons flour
- ½ teaspoon salt
- ¼ teaspoon pepper
- ½ cup sherry (optional)
- 1 cup cream

Sauté the mushrooms over a low heat. When the edges turn brown, remove to a warm dish. Sprinkle flour into the pan, stirring until butter, mushroom juices, and flour become smooth and thick. Add salt and pepper and continue cooking. This is important because uncooked flour in a subtle dish such as this one actually imparts a flour taste. Before the flour browns from the heat, add the half cup of sherry (optional), and simmer until most of the liquid has evaporated. Add the cream and stir until it reaches the desired thickness. Then, put in the sauteed mushrooms, and reheat them. Serve on toasted, home-made white bread. A great meal. One difficult to eat without becoming gluttonous.

Eat, drink, and be merry. Summer will be upon us, and it will be a long time before November's browns and gray. Rejoice and revel in the rich bounties of nature!

Chapter 7
June

*"Nature's first green is gold,
Her hardest hue to hold...."*

Robert Frost

June. Here it comes. Warm days, and warmer, but seldom hot. Blue skies, drifting puffs of cumulus clouds, and verdant countryside greener than it ever gets. Robert Frost must have been thinking of this month when he penned the above couplet. As summer moves toward autumn, foliage fades and fields turn rich yellow. Green wanes.

This month, bass fishing gets as good as it ever will. There will be plenty of these white-fleshed fighters to prepare into epicurean delights. Of course, white perch, yellow perch, sunfish, and pickerel may be substituted. One of the world's most prized and delectable fruits, strawberries, will be found in rich soil in fields and along roadsides. Cat-tails, a plant one naturalist called "the supermarket of the swamps", are at their best this month. We eat three different parts of a cat-tail plant, and love it. Truly. It is somewhat bland, not offensive at all. Also, it is reassuring for us to know one acre of cat-tails produces more food than an acre of wheat, corn, or rice! In the event of a global holocaust, we do not intend to starve. There's a lot of food out there—free for anyone willing to get it.

The making of a fine meal. Photo courtesy of Maine Department of Inland Fisheries and Wildlife.

DEEP-FRIED BASS

A good, old-fashioned Southern fish fry begins with a cast-iron deep fryer, and some mail-order businesses in this country do a brisk business selling this item. The important thing in this cooking is the proper temperature of cooking oil. It should be 380-390°. If it is cooler, the batter becomes leathery and greasy rather than a golden-crisp joy.

First, gather the following ingredients:

    bass, whole or filet
1 cup flour
1 teaspoon salt
⅛ teaspoon pepper
2 lightly beaten eggs
1 cup bread crumbs

If the bass are large enough, filet them. Boneless fish is a joy. If not, whole ones are great. It's free and fresh. Plan on ¼-pound of filets for each person, or a pound of whole fish. These are not hardcore rules. We won't admit how many fish we have polished off during one of these fish orgies.

Put the flour, salt, and pepper in a brown paper bag, and shake, mixing ingredients. Beat two eggs lightly. Lay the bread crumbs on a plate. Heat the oil in a Dutch oven until it is between 380-390°. Have enough oil so the fish will be submerged in it. When the fish are done, they will bob to the top and float. Remove them immediately. That is a good rule of thumb.

Drop the fish into the bag with the flour, shake the bag, coating the pieces. Remove, dip into the egg batter, then roll in the bread crumbs. Slip carefully into the fat and remove when done. Serve this meal with French fries, cole slaw, buttermilk biscuits, and beer. A meal as American as apple pie, and Chevrolets.

SAUTÉED BASS

Simplicity in itself. You need two or three tablespoons of butter, half-cup of flour, salt, and pepper. A cast-iron frying pan rounds things out. Rub the cavity and outside of the bass (white perch, pickerel, etc. will work fine) with salt. Really scour it. Sprinkle on pepper. Then, over a medium heat, get the butter sizzling. While waiting, dredge the fish lightly in flour. Lay the fish into the sizzling butter without crowding them, then reduce heat to medium-low. When one side is brown, about four minutes with a regular pan-sized fish, turn, and brown the other. When the meat flakes easily from the bone, and is still moist (not translucent), serve with a lemon wedge or maybe drenched with the butter and juices from the pan. Anything that pleases. Sautéed bass is a democratic dish.

BAKED BASS

This recipe is for the lucky angler who takes a three-to-five-pound bass. Eviscerate and remove pectoral and ventral fins, but leave the head (minus the gills) intact. Juices are lost when a fish is baked without the head or tail. It goes without saying the scales should be removed.

Next, rub vigorously with salt. Rub the inside well and take special care with the outside scouring. You may want to stuff the fish. Try this stuffing:

- **3 tablespoons butter**
- **¾ cup chopped onions**
- **¾ cup sliced mushrooms**
- **¾ cup cracker crumbs**
- **½ teaspoon salt**
- **¼ teaspoon pepper**
- **¼ teaspoon dill weed (optional)**
- **just enough milk to dampen the stuffing**

Sauté the mushrooms and onions over a low heat. When the onions first turn translucent, remove and put the mushrooms, onions, butter, and juices in a bowl. Add the crackers, salt, pepper, and dill weed, and mix. If it is really dry, just spill in some milk, a tablespoon at a time, until it is moist. All we care about is moist crackers. Sometimes, if the mushrooms are watery, no milk is needed. Stuff the fish.

Lay the fish on a shallow baking pan; brush heavily with melted butter and lemon juice. For every four tablespoons of melted butter, add a half tablespoon of lemon juice. A good combination. After the basting, put into a preheated 375° oven for approximately 10–12 minutes per pound. Every 10 minutes, baste with the melted butter and lemon. When done, the meat along the bone will have turned from translucent to opaque. Serve with French bread, mashed potatoes, tossed garden salad, and frenched string beans. Baked fish, whether it is bass or the lordly salmon, really reaches epic proportions. Enjoy one of June's best bounties.

Anything that may be cooked at home in a Dutch oven may be cooked over coals. Here, biscuits are baking. Ken Allen photo.

BASS SALAD

This is an interesting recipe for a hot summer day. Since the fish are poached and boned, the recipe particularly lends itself to perch and pickerel. Lay the cleaned fish in a Dutch oven, barely cover with water, throw in a quartered onion and quartered celery stalk, sprinkle in a teaspoon of salt, and bring to a smiling boil over a medium-low heat. Reduce heat and simmer until the flesh along the backbone turns from translucent to opaque, and flakes easily. Remove fish from broth and cool. Then, bone the fish. We take pride in boning fish. We dislike one bone or fleck of skin to elude us.

For each cup of clear meat, chop two tablespoons of onions and two tablespoons of celery. The finer you chop these vegetables, the better. Mix with the fish, salt and pepper to taste, and then add enough mayonnaise to make a moist salad just like tuna fish—only better. It's fresh and free. Place in the refrigerator for a few hours to get it good and cold and to allow the onion and celery flavoring to permeate the meat. Serve as sandwiches or on fresh beds of lettuce. Garnish with paprika and parsley. This just could start a tradition.

BASS CHOWDER

Once in a while in summer, days turn raw. During these unseasonable cold spells, a chowder goes well. Use the recipe in Chapter 2. The white, flaky meat of bass particularly lends itself to chowders. We promise.

ROLLED-STUFFED FILETS

This is a perfect meal for special guests. It is so festive, calling for a good bottle of French Chablis. It is simple to prepare, freeing you to entertain a little between dashes to the kitchen. First, you need a stuffing. This one is perfect. It is a delightful balance between lightness and richness.

Gourmet Seafood Stuffing

Gather the following ingredients:

    2 packages Waverly Wafers
    ¼ pound butter
    2 tablespoons vinegar
    1–2 tablespoons sherry
        parsley
    4 heaping tablespoons of grated
        cheese (parmesan, Swiss, Cheddar, or Gruyère)
        paprika for color

This recipe is actually for baked-stuffed shrimp, but is perfect for this festive meal. The Waverly Wafers make it rich, but still light.

Crush the crackers finely, then combine with the melted butter, sherry, and vinegar. Mix thoroughly, and set aside. Grate the cheese. When ready to use this stuffing, whether it is for baked-stuffed shrimp or baked-stuffed halibut, spread it on and sprinkle with grated cheese, parsley, and paprika.

For these rolled-stuffed filets, take each serving piece, pat it dry, and lay it flat. This recipe is for bass filets, but if you are not fortunate enough to catch a fish this large, any filet will do—flounder, cusk, or anything you can get. Spread the stuffing on the filet, sprinkle on the cheese, parsley, and paprika, and roll like a jelly roll. Secure with a toothpick. Bake in a 400° preheated oven for 30 minutes. While the fish cooks, grate more cheese to add onto the tops of these little delights. Remove at the end of 30 minutes, sprinkle with cheese, and put back into the oven for an additional 10 minutes, or until the fish flakes easily. Don't overcook. Serve with French bread, broccoli, rice pilaf, and a tossed garden salad. It is a festive enough meal for French Chablis, so splurge. It is a superior time of year.

GRILLED EEL

Let's face it. Eels do not look appetizing to a lot of folks. Us included. So, we keep telling ourselves three things. Eels are plentiful, easy to catch, and yes, revered in Europe. And, you might say those people know something about good food. Why not give it a try?

Skin, clean, and cut about three pounds of eel into two-to-three-inch pieces. Get a court bouillon heated to a smiling bubble. Slide in the chunks of eel, and simmer for 15–20 minutes. Remove the pot from the heat and let the pieces of eel cool right in the liquid. Whether it is braised red meat or fish, it is better to allow it to cool in a broth. It makes the meat moister. Truly. When the eel has cooled completely, remove from the bouillon, and pat completely dry with a paper towel. Dip the pieces in.melted butter, roll in bread crumbs, and broil under a preheated broiler or over medium-dark coals. Turn so they will brown on all sides, and serve with tartar sauce, wine, and rye bread. It is possible you may feel no fish ever tasted better.

EELS IN BEER

Clean, skin, and cut eels into three-inch chunks. Then, gather the following ingredients.

- 3–4 pounds eel chunks
- 24 ounces beer, preferably dark
- 2 onions, chopped
- ½ lemon sliced
- 1 bay leaf
- ½ teaspoon dill weed (optional)
- melted butter for dipping fish

This meal is best cooked outside over a campfire. Beer and fish make an odor! In a Dutch oven, gently pour the beer. As little head as possible, please. Add the chopped onions, sliced lemon, bay leaf, and dill weed. Slip in the chunks of eel, place on a fire, and bring to a boil. Slide it away from the heat and simmer for 15 or 20 minutes, or until the meat turns from translucent to opaque. Serve with melted butter for dipping the chunks. Beer seems to complement this meal.

COAL-BROILED EEL

Simplicity in itself. Build a hardwood fire. While it burns to coals, clean some eels, leaving the skins on. Find yourself a green alder stick, sharpen it on one end, and skewer a chunk of eel. Broil until done. The skin helps keep the meat moist. A favorite meal of Indians in Northern New England and the Maritime provinces. Maybe it will be with you.

DEEP-FRIED HORNPOUT

A four-foot board, pliers, nail hammer, and nails make short work of cleaning hornpout. Lean the board against a shed wall, nail the fish's head to it, make an incision around the head below the gills, peel back the skin a little, grab with pliers, and pull. With a few cuts, you will have a piece of red-fleshed fish, sometime even redder than salmon! If the hornpout are large enough, filet. With practice and a sharp knife, it only takes minutes to clean a mess of 'pouts.

Once cleaned and ready for cooking, proceed exactly as you would with the deep-fried bass recipe. This meal could really start a family tradition. Serve with beer and anything else your heart desires. Hornpout makes a very democratic fish, as American as the 4th of July. Hornpout makes an excellent chowder also. Give that a try.

COLD STRAWBERRY SOUP

Delightful on a hot day. Gather the following ingredients:

- 4 cups ripe strawberries
- 1 cup sugar
- 1 cup sour cream
- 1 cup sherry
- touch of nutmeg
- 2 cups of water (more if you want thinner soup)

Put the strawberries through a fine sieve. Mix the mash with sugar, sour cream, sherry, nutmeg, and water. We like a thick soup. You be the judge. We like two cups of water. You may like as many as four. On a low heat, bring this mixture to a near boil, stirring constantly with a whip. Don't let it boil. Remove just below the boiling point and chill. We have seen folks use this as an appetizer, but we like cold strawberry soup just fine by itself on a hot afternoon. A delightful treat—one that may be made with raspberries, blackberries, or even blueberries.

SAUTÉED CAT-TAIL STEMS

All cat-tail stalks have a tough, outer-green layer. Cut the stalk and peel this layer back to a crisp white core. It sort of resembles the texture and feel of cucumber. Early in the season when the plant is one-to-three-feet high, cut it near the ground. As the season progresses, the core is more tender by the upper leaves. It takes a little experimenting to become proficient at choosing the proper spot to peel the stalk.

When you have peeled enough stems, around 10, four-to-six-inches long, slice thinly, and sauté in butter over a medium-low heat until tender. If you mix the sliced cat-tail stems with chopped onions and sliced mushrooms, and sauté together, this side dish begins to approach gourmet proportions. And, cat-tails are plentiful and free. What more can we ask?

STEAMED CAT-TAIL STEMS

Gather 26 cat-tail stems four-to-six-inches long. Put them in a steaming basket, dot with two tablespoons of butter, sprinkle on a half-teaspoon salt, a quarter-teaspoon pepper, and bring to a boil. When it starts steaming, cook 20–30 minutes, or until the cat-tail pieces are tender. Use a low heat so the pot won't go dry. Serve with butter, baked fish, buttered, boiled potatoes, and white wine.

BOILED CAT-TAIL FLOWERS

Relax. We do not eat the flower when it is brown. In June, the green, immature flower spike can be eaten as a boiled veggie, and it is excellent. Collect a dozen or so, remove the papery husk, and boil the inner part in salted water for a few minutes. This does not take long because we eat just the outside of this vegetable just like an ear of corn. As soon as the outside becomes tender, serve with melted butter, lightly seasoned with a touch of garlic powder. Be careful with the garlic though. This is a dish somewhat bland. Not offensive at all. You will be pleasantly surprised, and may become a flower spike aficionado. Of course, this is a side dish that goes with nearly anything.

One way or the other, it is June. Heaven on Earth. Eat, drink, and smile. It is a grand life. Some of the world's finest foods are available to us, and they're free. We appreciate that. Truly.

Salmon ascending the river of their birth. Atlantic salmon epitomize the life-force. Photo courtesy of Maine Department of Inland Fisheries and Wildlife.

Chapter 8
July

July. Blue skies. Drifting cumulus clouds and thunderheads building in the distance. Sun, sun, and more sun blazing across summer landscape. Everything shimmers under it...hayfields, blueberry barrens, beaches, waters, and forests. It's July. A month not a month, but a season within itself. Intoxicating.

Tradition dictates salmon, peas, boiled potatoes, and biscuits for the Fourth of July. An honorable American custom. Beyond that, culinary variety is the name of the game this time of year. Clams are plentiful, and we better get a few feeds before the red tide. Gardens begin massive yields of early vegetables. Spinach, peas, string beans, and summer squash pile up on the back porches or pantry counters. Strawberry season begins to wind down, but raspberry patches are laden with fruit. Bass are still biting, and the backyard grill is as ready as it ever gets for barbecued ribs. Maybe there are some bear or deer ribs in the freezer. If not, supermarkets stock up on spareribs during the summer. Not a bad substitute. Nature has some other free offerings. Two are gourmet delights. Underutilized ones at that. Frog's legs and crayfish are wonderful delicacies. Wild carrots are everywhere this month, and everyone can recognize this veggie. Most of us call it Queen Anne's Lace.

THOMAS JEFFERSON BOILED POTATOES

Boiled potatoes are an integral part of a Fourth of July dinner, but like all simple foods, an extra touch brings them to legendary proportions, and you along with it...at least in your family...where legends count. Allegedly, Tom Jefferson preferred his boiled potatoes in the following manner, and even wrote about it. We tried his method, and must agree. In education and cooking, Thomas Jefferson knew his stuff.

Whether the potatoes are peeled or in their jackets is your choice. We peel them. In a pot, preferably of cast-iron, we put enough potatoes to serve the guests. Then, we add one-to-two teaspoons of salt, enough cold water to cover the potatoes, then place the pot on a high heat. As soon as it begins to boil, the heat is reduced to medium-low; 30–40 minutes later, when the potatoes are tender, the water is dumped out, then the pot placed back on the stove. Leave it there for two or three minutes, shaking occasionally, until the potatoes are dry. It makes such a difference.

BUTTERED-PARSLEYED POTATOES

Boil the potatoes in the above manner. While this cooks, melt a tablespoon of butter for each potato. Lightly season the butter with garlic powder. Butter is easily flavored, so be careful. Not more than a pinch for every four tablespoons. When the potatoes are done, pour the butter over them and garnish with snipped fresh parsley.

FOURTH OF JULY SALMON

Sometimes, salmon come hard during the warmer months. Plan on having one in the freezer, just in case. Use May's recipe for Poached Salmon, the traditional method for the Fourth. Serve this with buttered-parsleyed potatoes, biscuits, and fresh peas. Salmon does not call for a great wine, and we usually serve a white Bordeaux, Graves to be exact. But, it's the Fourth, so be patriotic and serve a California Sauvignon Blanc. If you caught the salmon, and the peas and potatoes are from your garden, and the butter on your biscuits from your churn, eat, drink, and have a grand and glorious day. You have a right to smugly wonder what the rich people are doing.

FRESH GARDEN PEAS

If you were able to work the soil in the garden early enough to get the peas in by Patriot's Day, chances are good that fresh peas will be on the table by the Fourth.

In a pot, preferably cast-iron, heat a half-inch of water to boiling, stir in a tablespoon of salt, and put in the young, tender peas. Put a dollop of butter on top, and bring to a boil again. Reduce heat to low, and simmer uncovered for five minutes. Cover and cook until the peas just become tender. Be careful, and don't overcook. It may only take two or three minutes after covering.

STEAMED CLAMS

The poor man's lobster. How we love 'em, particularly when we have dug them. Like any seafood, clams should never be overcooked. This only toughens the flesh. Properly cooked steamed clams are a succulent delight. A friend of ours claims to be a real clam chef. We agree with his claim. He feels there is only one way to determine if a clam is done properly. There is a small, cylindrical muscle that attaches the clam and shell. If the clams are not overdone or underdone, this tiny, white piece will come off when the clam is removed. This fellow has cooked us many clam feeds at his house, usually over an open fire, and they are usually done to his specifications.

If we have a large batch of clams, we like to use a turkey roaster and two burners, or an open fire. This spreads the clams out more and they cook better. The clams on bottom are less apt to be overdone, and the ones on top won't be raw. Put a half-inch of water on the bottom of the cooking utensil, and lightly salt. Make sure the clams are cleaned well—preferably each one scrubbed with a brush. It is so hard to get rid of the grit. Bring the water to a boil, add the clams, and wait for it to boil again. Make sure the pot is covered. When it boils again, cook until all the clams are open, about 10 minutes. Remove immediately to serving dishes. Clams will continue to cook just from the heat of their shells, so don't add to it by leaving them in the hot broth.

Serve clams with a dish of clam broth and melted butter. A touch of vinegar in the butter allegedly aids the digestive process. Clams are difficult little critters sometimes. We think the vinegar helps. Of course, the clam broth is for dipping the shucked clam to remove that inevitable grit.

Stan Foye takes advantage of nature's bounty. He digs his own clams . . . year after year. Ken Allen photo.

CLAM CHOWDER

Nothing beats clam chowder on chilled, rainy days. We have a simple, time-honored recipe with a few secrets of our own. First, gather the following ingredients:

- 1 quart shucked clams
- 1 cup lightly salted water
- ¼ pound cubed salt pork
- 1 large onion, chopped
- 1½ potatoes, cooked and cubed, for each serving
- 1½ pints clam broth
- 1 pint cream
- 1 teaspoon salt
- ½ teaspoon pepper
- ¼ teaspoon thyme (optional)

Steam the clams in the shell. The recipe calls for a quart of shucked clams, and we realize that is a pile of them. This really varies with the cook's whim. A pint of clams would suffice. When you cook these clams, have them slightly undercooked. Remember, they will cook some more in the chowder. Save the broth.

Next, brown the salt pork in a Dutch oven, preferably a cast-iron one. Brown well over a medium heat, and let them crust the pot's bottom a little. Remove the browned pieces and all but two or three tablespoons of fat. Turn the heat to medium-low and lightly brown the onion. Turn the heat up to medium-high, and dump the clam broth in. It will really sizzle. With a wooden spoon, scrape the crust from the pan's bottom. Then, reduce the heat to medium-low. Add the seasonings and simmer for a few minutes. Add the cooked, cubed potatoes and clams, and heat through. Remove from heat, and add the cream. Cream is one of the secrets of a superior clam chowder. Reheat the chowder.

If you have used a quart of clams, one-and-a-half potatoes for each person, and our recommended amounts of liquid, you should have a chowder that is tempting to eat with a fork. But you won't because the broth is a big part of clam chowder. Serve with biscuits or home-made crackers and plenty of tea or coffee.

FRIED CLAMS

There is a lot of work to this dish, but the reward will be an appreciative family. Gather the following ingredients:

- **1 pint shucked, fresh clams**
- **1 cup flour**
- **1 teaspoon salt**
- **dash pepper**
- **2 eggs, straight from refrigerator**
- **3 tablespoons ice water**
- **1½ cups dry bread crumbs**
- **vegetable oil for deep frying**

Drain the fresh, shucked clams. Put a cup of flour, teaspoon of salt, and dash of pepper in bag, and shake, mixing ingredients. Drop the clams into the bag, and shake, coating them well. You may want to do this in steps instead of all at once. Shake excess flour from clams, and dip them into a mixture made from the eggs and ice water. Roll in bread crumbs and place in oil heated to 375°. When golden brown, remove, let excess oil run off completely, set on paper bag or towels for a moment, then serve with french fries, cole slaw, home-made yeast rolls, and plenty of tartar sauce. Cold beer goes great.

BROILED CLAMS

We have to throw this recipe in. It is ancient and certainly honorable. Once, wandering a secluded cove with a special friend, we noticed a profusion of tell-tale holes in a mudflat. We dug a couple dozen clams by hand, washed them in the Atlantic's chill water, and built a small fire below tide line. When it burned down, we began laying clams directly on the coals. With nothing but green sticks for utensils, we would carefully lift them from the coals as soon as the shell opened, trying not to spill the juice. We ate these plain, and washed them down with sips of Moselle wine from a bottle we had brought along. A memorable meal. So memorable. Why are the simple, primitive meals like that?

The fruits of the ocean's harvest. Stan Foye cooks fresh clams that he dug during the morning. Ken Allen photo.

CLAM CAKES

Home-made clam cakes are becoming a thing of the past. What a shame! They are an epicurean delight in comparison to the frozen variety from the local supermarket. Gather the following ingredients:

- 1 pint fresh, shucked clams chopped finely
- ¼ cup clam juice from shucked clams
- ¾ cup unsifted flour
- 1 teaspoon baking powder
- ¼ cup milk
- 1 egg
- ¼ teaspoon black pepper
- ½ teaspoon salt
- 1 heaping tablespoon grated onion
- cayenne pepper (optional)

Beat the clam juice, flour, baking powder, milk, egg, pepper, and salt until it has made a smooth batter. Add the clams and onions and stir. Let stand for 10 minutes. Melt four tablespoons of butter over a medium-low heat. When the butter begins to bubble, drop spoonfuls of the batter onto the hot pan. When it browns well on one side, turn, and brown the other side well. Serve with French fries, cole slaw, tartar sauce, and cold lager beer.

BARBECUE SAUCE

This is a fine recipe we have had good luck with. It makes a large quantity, but it may be frozen for later. Gather the following ingredients:

- 3 pounds stewed tomatoes
- 1 pint water
- 1 cup vinegar
- ¼ cup dark brown sugar
- 3 crushed garlic cloves
- 1 crushed bay leave
- juice of one lemon
- 1 teaspoon oregano
- 1 teaspoon chili powder
- ½ teaspoon dry mustard
- 2 onions, grated

In a Dutch oven, preferably cast-iron, put the tomatoes, water, vinegar, brown sugar, crushed garlic cloves, bay leaf, lemon juice, oregano, chili powder, and dry mustard. Place pot on a low heat, and bring to a gentle bubble. While it is heating, grate in the onions, juice and all. Once it starts to bubble, cook for at least an hour. When done, remove the bay leaf, and let the sauce set. It improves with age.

BARBECUED RIBS

Bear or deer ribs really become special over coals. If you have none, spare ribs work just fine. Before barbecueing ribs, bring a pot of water to a rapid boil, and drop the ribs in. When it begins to boil again, lower heat, cook for five minutes, and remove ribs. This is done solely to remove a little fat.

Some folks advocate simmering meat for 30 minutes, claiming it keeps the barbecueing time less, consequently, keeping the meat from blackening. Their theory seems plausible. An hour of cooking may blacken the outside, where the inside may be pink, a real problem with bear or pork. When people say this, we shudder. We have few pet peeves about cooking, but this is one.

The secret to a superior barbecue is work! We turn the meat constantly, brushing on sauce each time, never allowing the outside to get black! The finished ribs will be moist and succulent, but still cooked, and the outside will be reddish-brown, and almost crispy.

Serve ribs with potatoes and onions broiled in foil, garden salad, corn bread, and beer.

CRAYFISH BOILED IN BEER

Never...ever...have we been able to figure out why crayfish are not a popular food in this country. Folks associate crayfish with the South or Europe. The truth is these delectable creatures abound in northern lakes. You do not see them that often because they are nocturnal. However, go out after dark to just about any body of water, shine a flashlight on the bottom, and sooner or later, you will see crayfish.

We go out after dark with a short, stiff rod with a string with meat attached on the end. We throw the meat out, shine a flashlight on it, and if it is good crayfish water, soon, a crayfish will crawl over. We wait until they begin to back up with the bait, then with a steady, firm tug, snap them onto the bank. In no time at all, we'll have a pot full.

This is definitely a gourmet food, sweet and subtle. Our most memorable meals have been simple affairs, however. We get a Coleman stove burning on the tailgate of our truck, get an inch of beer boiling, and dump in the crayfish whole and alive—just like lobster. Just as soon as they turn pink, dump out the broth and serve. The cooking time is seldom more than three to five minutes once the beer starts to boil again. Dip them in melted butter, and enjoy one of nature's finest foods. It's free, and better yet, plentiful.

Any recipe that works for shrimp will be great for crayfish. You may like them so well you will make traps from heavy mesh wire. The traps will look exactly like a bait trap. Put a weight and bait in a trap, hook a rope to it, sink it in a likely spot, tie a buoy to the rope, and come back a day later. The bait should be a rotten piece of fish, or even a sardine can unopened, but poked with holes. The results of this endeavor quite often are a trap full of epicurean delights.

SAUTÉED FROG'S LEGS

As children, we ate quite a few meals of frog's legs. When people think of frogs, they usually think of the smaller species like the leopard frog or green frog, certainly edible, but tiny. The frogs we ate were giant bull frogs, over half-a-foot long. Cleaning them was simple. We merely cut the legs off, and peeled the skin back, exposing light-pink meat that turned as white as a chicken breast in the frying pan.

After skinning the legs, soak them for a half-hour in a quart of water and two tablespoons salt. Before getting ready to cook them, gather the following ingredients:

- 1 **cup flour**
- ½ **teaspoon salt**
- ¼ **teaspoon pepper**
- 2 **eggs, slightly beaten**
- 1 **cup of extra-fine bread crumbs**
- 4 **tablespoons butter**

Pat the legs dry after the soaking. Put them in a paper bag with the cup of flour, salt, and pepper, and shake, coating the legs thoroughly. Remove from bag, shake excess flour off, and dip into the egg. Let excess egg run off, and roll in bread crumbs. Shake off excess bread crumbs. All this precaution just so the coating won't be thick, overpowering the tiny legs. Over a medium-low heat, melt the butter, and bring it to a bubble. Don't brown it. Lay the legs into the butter, and brown. Serve as an appetizer with a good white wine, dry, of course. If you can overcome built-in prejudices against eating this food, you'll find its meat is white, succulent, and sweet. A gourmet's delight. Really. And, the best part of it all, it is free, abundant, and folks are not exactly overutilizing the resource.

SUMMER SQUASH CASSEROLE

When boiled summer squash begins to become unbearable, try this wonderful dish. Gather the following ingredients:

- 3 **pounds summer squash**
- ½ **cup chopped onions**
- ½ **cup cracker crumbs**
- 2 **eggs**
- 1 **stick butter**
- 1 **teaspoon salt**
- ¼ **teaspoon pepper**

Boil the sliced squash until tender, drain thoroughly, and then mash. Add all the ingredients except half the butter and all the crumbs. Pour mixture into buttered baking dish, spread, then cover with remainder of butter. Sprinkle on bread crumbs, and bake for one hour in 375° oven. This meal goes well with barbecued deer or bear ribs and beer. It is excellent, quite piquant with a distinctive onion flavor.

WILD CARROTS

Most folks can recognize wild carrots. They just know them by another name—Queen Anne's Lace. Most of us can easily identify this plant, but just one word of caution. It bears a faint resemblance to poison hemlock. Very faint. There should be no problem. Just remember wild carrot has a stem covered with hair, where poison hemlock has a smooth stem with purple spots. It is interesting to note, if you leave domestic carrots in the ground, the next spring, a flower will form on the carrot plants that looks like Queen Anne's Lace. That should tell you something. If you want large, mature roots, gather them in the fall or spring, just as with the domestic. However, one way or the other, gather a bunch of them. They smell unmistakably like carrot, but are white like parsnips. If you get a hodge-podge of sizes, clean them, peel, and put them in a pot with a half-inch of salted water, a half-teaspoon to the cup, and a dollop of butter. Put on a medium heat and bring to a boil. Reduce heat and cook until tender. In September's chapter, when you get some mature wild carrots, we'll give you a recipe for brandied carrots. Sinfully good.

COLD RASPBERRY SOUP

In the June chapter, there is a recipe for Cold Strawberry Soup. This month, when the raspberry patches are producing and this berry is coming out of your ears, make a Cold Raspberry Soup in the same manner as you might have with the strawberries. Delightful.

July. It's a grand way of life. Need we say more.

Wild plants offer a cornucopia of foods for the person willing to harvest them. Ken Allen photo.

Katie Sutton picks her own home-grown carrots.   Ken Allen photo.

Chapter 9
August

August. Here it comes. A glaring, relentless sun and haze on the horizon. Gardens look powder-dry and lawns turn golden-brown. A few swamp maples, sumac, and blueberry bushes turn red, and days shorten, signs of the coming autumn, but only astute observers notice. Heat is the immediate problem. You are unable to escape it during the day. Just in dawn's early hours. A little relief.

Heat or not...this is a grand month for cooking. We particularly love to eat any food cooked over coals. The kitchen is hot anyway, and what better excuse to leave it than an outdoor barbecue. Seafood is plentiful this month. Sports fishermen are bringing home mackerel, stripers, and blues. Seafood markets, catering to tourists, are laden, and on the coast, you might be able to buy some fish directly from fishing boats. Mackerel and blues, somewhat oily, reach gargantuan proportions as epicurean delights when grilled over coals. Basted with butter or other sauces, the succulent, white-fleshed seafoods more popular with American palates are superior over a good bed of smokeless coals. Gardens really are producing this month. Brassica plants should be coming from your ears. There are still string beans, and yes, finally, one of the New World's most prized gifts is ready—corn! Crayfish are still active and plentiful, and who could tire of this delicacy. Blueberries and blackberries are ripe, and ready. Fresh food is everywhere. Rejoice. It's still summertime, and living is easy....

GRILLED MACKEREL

Simplicity. All you need are two mackerel per person, and a butter sauce made from one stick of melted butter, a pinch of salt, a tiny pinch of garlic powder, and a half-tablespoon of fresh lemon juice. Split the mackerels' backs so they can lie flat on the grill.

When the coals become medium-dark, lay the mackerel on a grill five inches from the coals. Place them so the skin side is up. Cook four to seven minutes, depending on the size, flip over, and baste lightly. Cook an additional four to seven minutes. When the meat flakes easily from the bone, and is still moist, serve with lemon wedges. A fresh garden salad, corn-on-the-cob, and beer make this a typical summer delight.

MUSTARD-BUTTER GRILLED MACKEREL

An interesting recipe that makes a hit with guests. Gather the following ingredients:

- 2 mackerel per person
- 1 stick melted butter
- 2 tablespoons Dijon mustard
- ½ tablespoon fresh lemon juice
- ¼ teaspoon salt
- ⅛ teaspoon pepper

Mix the butter, Dijon mustard, lemon juice, salt, and pepper, and let it sit for 20–30 minutes. Split the mackerels' backs. When the coals are medium-dark, grease the broiler rack well, place five inches from the coals, and lay the fish on, skin-side up. Broil four to seven minutes, turn, and baste with the butter-mustard sauce. Cook an additional four to seven minutes, or until the flesh along the bone begins to flake easily. Of course, the cooking time depends entirely on the size of the mackerel, so keep an eagle eye.

GRILLED BLUEFISH STEAKS

Prepare the bluefish by cutting it into one-inch steaks. Prepare a butter sauce to lightly baste the steaks while grilling. It is made exactly like the sauce for grilled mackerel. Melt a stick of butter, and add a pinch of salt, a tiny pinch of garlic powder, and a half-tablespoon of lemon juice. When the coals are medium-bright, grease a grill, and set it five inches from the coals. Lay the steaks on, baste lightly, and cook four minutes per side, or until the flesh flakes easily. Serve with corn-on-the-cob, tossed garden salad, and lots of ice-cold beer.

GRILLED STRIPER FILETS IN ITALIAN DRESSING

A piquant recipe, ideal for this species of fish. Simplicity in itself. Take enough striper filets to feed your guests, and marinade them in Italian dressing for 15 minutes. Any commercial dressing will work, as long as it is not creamy Italian. Of course, if you are a purist, you will make your own dressing.

Over medium-dark coals, set a well-greased grill so the fish will be five inches from the heat. Lay on the filets, and cook three to four minutes per side, depending on size. If they are thin filets, even a shorter cooking time. As soon as the meat turns from translucent to opaque, it is done. Baste lightly with the Italian dressing before turning.

Serve with corn-on-the-cob, a tossed garden salad, home-made white bread, and cold beer. This is a fish dish for finicky children.

BAKED STRIPER A LA TOMATOES

Serious striper fishermen catch a lot of pounds of fish in a season. This recipe is for the times folks need something more exotic. Take one bass of five or so pounds, or three pounds of thick filets, and prepare in the following manner. First, gather these ingredients.

juice of one lime or lemon
salt and pepper to taste
¼ **cup oil**
2 **cups chopped onions**
2 **tablespoons chopped garlic**
2 **1-pound cans of tomatoes**
1 **chopped green pepper**
1 **teaspoon oregano**
½ **teaspoon Tabasco sauce**

Sauté the onions, garlic, and peppers in olive oil. When lightly browned, add tomatoes, and bring to a smiling boil. Add the remainder of the ingredients (except for the lime or lemon juice). Simmer for an hour, or more. When ready to cook the striper, rub lime or lemon juice over it, including the cavity. Put the fish in a shallow baking dish, and dump on sauce. Bake uncovered in a 350° preheated oven.

SUPERB FISH BARBECUE RECIPE

This recipe is simple, and delightful. Most any fish will work, but it particularly lends itself to subtle, white-fleshed fish such as flounder, codfish, haddock, etc. It also may be cooked under a broiler as well as over coals. Gather the following ingredients:

> **6 fish filets, steaks, or
>   small, whole fish
> ½ cup oil
>   juice of two lemons
> ¼ teaspoon salt
>   dash of pepper**

Mix the oil, lemon juice, salt, and pepper. Lay the fish in a bowl, pour the oil mixture over them, and set bowl in the refrigerator for one hour. When ready to cook, have a bed of coals medium-dark, place a well-greased grill five inches from them, and lay on the fish. Cook three to five minutes per side, and turn. Baste before turning. Three to five minutes later, the fish should be done. Keep a careful eye on it though. Coals have such a variable heat.

GRILLED SOLE FILETS

When you have some delicate, white-fleshed filets such as flounder, try this recipe. It is simplicity plus. Gather the following ingredients:

> **fish filets
> ½ cup milk
> ½ cup flour
> ½ teaspoon salt
>   dash pepper
>   pinch of sage (optional)**

Pour the milk into a pie plate. In a paper bag, put the flour, salt, pepper, and sage, and shake to mix. When the coals are medium-dark, lay a well-greased grill five inches from the coals. Then, dip the fish pieces in milk, covering thoroughly, let excess milk drip off, then drop them into the bag of flour. Shake bag, coating the pieces. Shake off excess flour and lay on the grill. Cook three to four minutes per side, depending on size of filets. If you are unsure of cooking time, watch closely, and remove just as soon as fish flakes easily.

FISH FILETS POACHED IN WHITE WINE

This is an elegant recipe that may be prepared in an oven in your kitchen, or a reflector oven in front of a fire. The recipe is simple, needs little preparation, and looks so fancy. If you use a reflector oven, guests who have never seen one will be in awe. Gather the following ingredients:

- 4 filets
- 2 tablespoons soft butter
- 2 tablespoons melted butter
- ¾ cup of dry, white wine
- juice from one fresh lemon
- salt and pepper to taste
- 1 teaspoon dill weed (optional)

Smear two tablespoons soft butter on the bottom of a shallow baking dish. Dry filets with a paper towel, and lay them on the pan's bottom. Brush two tablespoons of melted butter on the filets, then sprinkle on lemon juice. Pour wine over the fish and sprinkle on salt, pepper, and dill weed. If you have never used dill weed, try it. The result is pleasing. Place in a 350° preheated oven, and bake until the filets turn from translucent to opaque. This meal calls for rice pilaf (cooked in a Dutch oven over coals), broccoli, French bread, and a great white wine. Meals this time of year are always excellent, but usually lend themselves to beer. This is a welcome change before the next carbohydrate orgy....

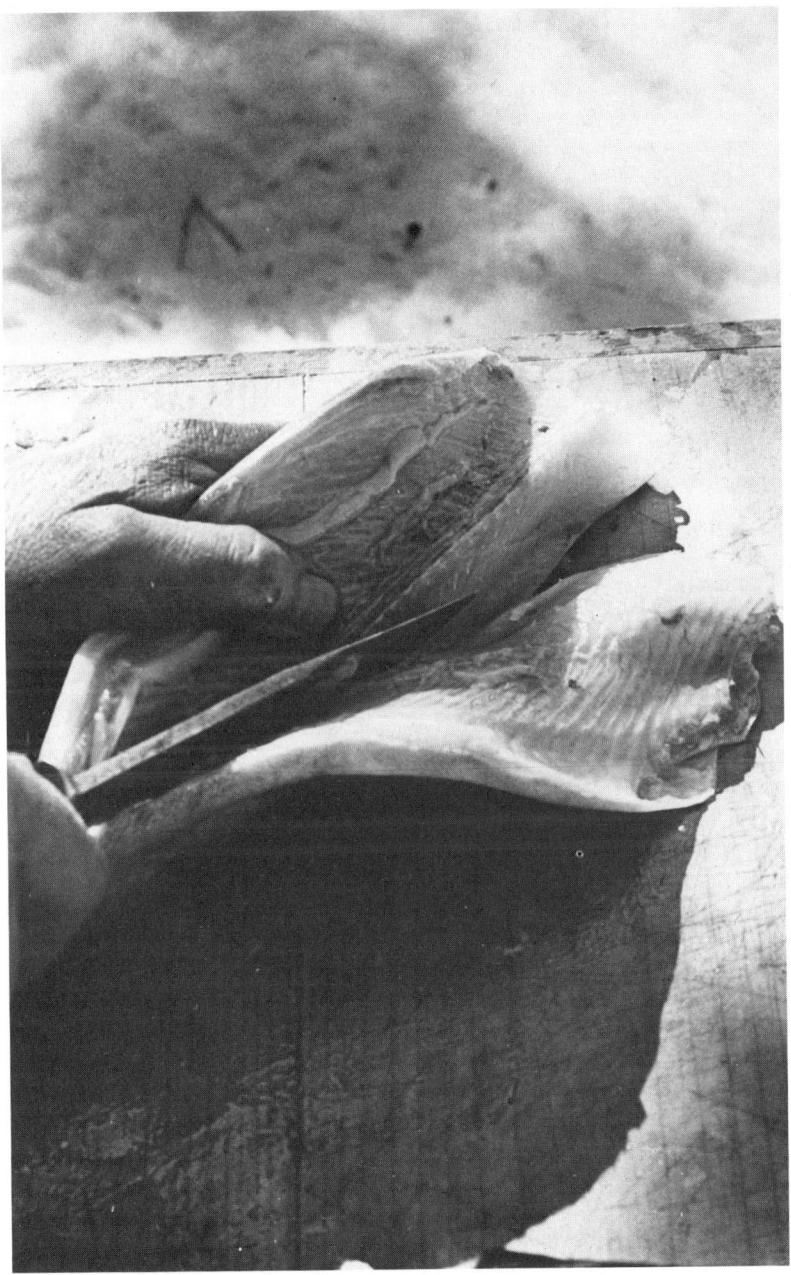

When the fish are big enough, filets are just the thing epicurean memories are made of. Photo courtesy of Maine Department of Inland Fisheries and Wildlife.

OLD-FAVORITE BAKED FISH RECIPE

The first time we ever saw this recipe was on Chamberlain Lake. A fellow sautéed a four-pound togue on a long griddle over a campfire. It took a long time to cook the fish, and the butter scorched, but we still ate a huge portion. The stuffing intrigued us, and still does. We use it for baked fish. Gather the following:

    1 four-to-five pound whole
       fish (striper, bass, togue, etc.)
    2 large onions, sliced
    2 green peppers, sliced
    4 tomatoes, sliced
       salt and pepper to taste
    ½ stick melted butter
       juice of one lemon
    ½ teaspoon dill weed

Clean the fish, leaving the head and tail attached. Make sure to remove gills. Slice onions, peppers, and tomatoes, and mix them in a bowl. Toss lightly so the tomatoes will not be beaten up. Salt and pepper to taste. You will need at least one teaspoon salt. Next, melt the butter; add lemon juice and dill weed. Lay the fish on a well-greased baking sheet, and stuff the cavity loosely. Lay the fish on its back and pour three quarters of the butter over the stuffing. Lay the fish on its side, baste the remainder of the butter on it, put the remainder of the vegetables (if any left) on top, and bake in a 375° preheated oven for 10–12 minutes per pound, or until meat flakes easily from the bone. Serve with buttered-parsleyed potatoes, cauliflower, home-made white bread, and a Bordeaux wine.

OVEN-FRIED FILETS

This is a simple recipe for any filet. Delicate, white-fleshed fish are really enhanced by this method. Gather the following:

    ½ cup flour
       dash of salt and pepper
    2 eggs, lightly beaten
    2 tablespoons milk or cream
    1 cup dry bread crumbs

Put the flour, salt, and pepper in a paper bag, and shake, mixing thoroughly. Beat the eggs and milk lightly. Pat filets dry and drop them into the bag. Shake. Then, dip the filets into the egg and milk mixture, then roll in bread crumbs. Lay these in a shallow baking dish that has a liberal amount of butter, and bake in a preheated 500° oven until the fish flakes easily, yet, is still moist and succulent. It shouldn't take longer than eight to twelve minutes, depending on the size of the pieces. Serve with mashed potatoes, frenched string beans, home-made white bread, and wine.

POTTED SHRIMP

This is an excellent recipe for appetizers, or those nights when cheese, crackers, and a spread are enough food. Potted is an ancient term for a method of food preservation before refrigerators made the scene. The following recipe may be cut in half, doubled, etc. Gather the following ingredients:

- **1 pound shelled shrimp (cooked)**
- **½ pound butter**
- **½ teaspoon salt**
- **½ teaspoon mace (optional)**

In a frying pan, clarify a half-pound of butter. If you plan on storing the potted shrimp for any length of time, clarify carefully, removing impurities. Then, finely chop the shrimp, and put equally into six small bowls. Next, blend the salt and mace (or any other herb that might suit your fancy) into the clarified butter. Pour the butter in equal portions over the shrimp. Wait for it to set, and serve with crackers, preferably, home-made crackers.

Any fish could be potted—even trout. It is interesting, and certainly an ancient and honorable method.

POTTED CRAYFISH

Prepare this dish exactly as you would potted shrimp, then, if you are devious enough, try to pass it off to guests and finicky family members as potted shrimp. It might start a family tradition....

CRAYFISH QUICHE

Quiche is an elegant meal, certainly one of the world's gourmet delights. Crayfish have a subtle flavor, complementing a good quiche. They go together very well. Besides that, this dish has another plus. There are nights when you may go "craw fishin' ", and not do well. All you need for a quiche filling is upwards to a cup of meat. Use the recipe in the December chapter, and then, if you really feel like impressing guests, cook it in a reflector oven. Even if it does not impress guests, it will keep the kitchen cool, and you outdoors.

COLD BLACKBERRY SOUP

Blackberries are big berries. It takes little time to pick a quart. If you want a change of pace from blackberry pies or dumplings, make a blackberry soup, and chill it. Use the recipe for Cold Strawberry Soup from the June chapter. Use the ripest berries possible, and serve this chilled delight as an entree before the Crayfish Quiche. Who'd believe life could be so good....

CORN-ON-THE COB

There's only one way to fully appreciate corn-on-the-cob, and that is to use really fresh corn. You must have a garden to get it as fresh as we like it. When we are ready for a corn feed, we set a Dutch oven on a medium-high heat. The pot will be about one-third full of cold water with a tablespoon of sugar added. We never salt the water. Some old-timer said it toughens corn.

Next, we saunter down to the garden, find as many ears as we need, and make a mental note of where they are. Then, in a rush and a tear, we pick them all at once, and run for the kitchen, beginning to husk the ears on the run. As soon as they are husked, we toss them into the water, which is boiling by then. When it begins to boil again, we reduce the heat and cook for seven or eight minutes until the corn is tender. We serve corn with butter, salt, and pepper, and anything else that suits our fancy. It goes with just about everything.

Katie Sutton picks her own home-grown corn.   Ken Allen photo.

Of course, our method of rushing from the garden is an exaggeration, but slight. Corn should be fresh. You really can tell the difference, even if it sets for an hour. The old-timer who told us about the salt claims the sugar in corn immediately turns to starch as soon as the ear is picked. We believe. It has to be fresh.

Once, we were explaining our corn-on-the-cob cooking method to a fellow from Florida. He said, "If you want it that fresh, why don't you just take a pot of boiling water into the garden and dump it on an ear...husk and all."

Straight-faced, we asked, "Do you really think it would cook?"

Corn cuisine is a serious endeavor...even when you're fooling....

COLD MASHED POTATO SALAD

Great potato salad for a change-of-pace dish. For each serving, peel one-and-a-half potatoes. Put in a pot, and cover slightly with cold water. Put in a half-teaspoon of salt, and bring to a boil. Reduce heat and cover at medium-low heat. Make sure to cover the pot during cooking. When potatoes are tender, dump the cooking water into a bowl, and save. Put the potatoes back on the heat for two to three minutes to dry them. Shake occasionally so they won't stick. This makes the mashed potatoes fluffier. Next, add a tablespoon of butter for every two potatoes, and mash. Next, instead of using milk, use the broth from the cooking. Add it slowly, until you have a nice, smooth mixture. Now, for every four potatoes, add a half chopped onion and a half green pepper. Salt and pepper to taste. This is a democratic dish. You may want to add pimentos, hot peppers, garlic powder, and your favorite herbs. Finely chopped celery or scallions are also great choices. Be creative. Chill the salad, and serve with a parsley and paprika garnish. Folks will be asking for seconds with this one.

SUMACADE

Sumacade was a favored drink of the North American Indians. They enjoyed it so much they gathered an abundance of berries, and dried them for winter. Evidently, they sweetened this beverage with honey, and made a drink similar to pink lemonade that was high in Vitamin C.

There is a little work to this ancient and honorable refreshment, but once you get set up, it is easier. The easy part is gathering berries. Sumac is easy to spot from a distance. The plant is big, 10 to 16 feet high, and the berry is dark red. The berries cluster, and really are visible. For every quart of sumacade, you need two cups of berries. It takes no time to gather this amount.

To make the sumacade, put two cups in a quart of cold water, and bruise and mash the berries until the water turns pink. Next, strain the juice through several layers of cheesecloth to remove the berries, and especially, the tiny hairs. The amount of sugar varies. These berries are extremely acidic sometimes; other times quite mild. Sugar to suit the palate. If you want a real treat, sweeten it with honey like the people who invented the drink.

August dog days can be miserable, but September and its promises of autumn's glories will come soon enough. In the meantime, August ain't half bad....

Chapter 10
September

September. Month of mellow fruitfulness. Glaring, sultry days have turned to mellifluous, cool jewels, sun-splashed under high, azure skies. Gardens bear staples for winter, and fields and forests, ladened with foods, fatten wildlife. Living seems easy, and simple, but there is an urgency in the air. Early frosts and scarlet swamp maples are a constant reminder.

This time of year, gardens are fulfilling. Root vegetables, the real staples of a garden, are finally ready. To the meat and potato culture of pod auger days, this was the reason for a garden. Greens, peas, even string beans were secondary trappings.

Before the first frost, we head to the garden with a wheelbarrow, and spend an afternoon gathering tomatoes, melons, pumpkins, and winter squash. Melons and pumpkins are novelty items, but tomatoes, and particularly squash, are staples. Appreciated. These foods pile up fast. We really feel as if we have done something.

There is sometimes an urgency in this first major harvesting. Sometimes it begins immediately after a weather forecast, predicting frost. Tomatoes and melons will be ruined. Some folks claim winter squash and pumpkins can take frost. The vines will die, but their fruits will be unhurt. We disagree. Where the frost has touched them, spoil spots will appear later. So we rush and gather everything before dark.

After the harvest moon with its inevitable frost, we go to the garden again. There is no hurry this time. We are after the root vegetables. They can wait....A week or two. Some of them can stay in the ground all winter. Leisurely, we dig potatoes, and pull carrots, onions, beets, and a few parsnips. We cover the rest of the parsnips with hay, and leave them. We need a few of these for deer stews. The rest of them will be better in spring.

Just from the garden, this month is an epicurean delight. But these days during seasonal transition offer much more. Cool weather improves the appetites of salmon and trout, and there is a flurry of fishing. There will be a few meals of fresh salmon and trout. Striped bass fishing hits a crescendo, and some of these will grace our table. Bear season begins. North American Indians relished this food, and we know some honest folks who will look us in the eye, and say they prefer it to venison, and even beef, particularly if the bear is young. We believe them. Bear is excellent. Also, this is the mushroom month. They are everywhere. We prefer meadow mushrooms, giant versions of store-bought mushrooms. They grow in pastures and are easy to identify. Mushrooms in the Boletus genus are plentiful, and some of these are truly gourmet mushrooms. It is a grand month for chefs.

BRAISED BEAR IN WINE

Pot roast is a common way to prepare bear meat. It tenderizes the meat, and since bear must be well-done like pork, nothing is lost. Gather the following ingredients:

- 1 roast, trimmed of fat
- 2–3 tablespoons oil or clarified butter
- 2 chopped onions
- 3 tablespoons flour
- 2 cups dry red wine
- 2 beef bouillon cubes
- 1 cup boiling water
- 3 whole cloves
- 1 heaping teaspoon salt
- ½ teaspoon pepper
- 2 cups small, whole carrots
- 1½ potatoes per person

Put a Dutch oven over a medium heat, and pour in two to three tablespoons of oil or clarified butter. Add the chopped onions and brown. Just as they begin to brown, put in the bear roast, and quickly sear on all sides. Push it to the side of the oven and sprinkle in three tablespoons of flour. Brown it. When it becomes browned and crusty, turn the heat to medium-high, wait a few moments, then dump in the wine. Scrape the flour from the pot's bottom, and stir it smooth. Add the cup of boiling water with two dissolved bouillon cubes, three cloves, salt, pepper, and reduce heat when it all boils. Reduce to low and simmer for two hours. An hour and 15 minutes before serving time, add the carrots and potatoes. By serving time, they should be good and tender, and the gravy rich and thickening. Serve with biscuits and tea or coffee.

BEAR STEW

Stew is a common method for serving bear meat. In a stew, it tastes pretty much like beef. Make a stew, using the *Venison Stew* recipe in the December chapter.

GRILLED BEAR RIBS

Bear ribs are every bit as good as spareribs. Use the *Barbecued Ribs* recipe from the July chapter.

BEAR ROAST

This recipe is for young, tender bear. You may enjoy it as much as roast beef; however, you must remember it has to be well-done. Trichinosis is a possibility with rare bear meat.

Trim excess fat, leaving a quarter inch. Season with black pepper and garlic powder. Lay on a rack in a shallow roasting pan, and bake in a 325° preheated oven. Cook a rib roast 35 minutes per pound; a ribless one 40 minutes per pound. However, for perfect results, this time method is unreliable. A meat thermometer will give consistent results. When it hits 170°, remove the roast. Bear meat must be well-done, but not cooked so long it is dry and tasteless. If this is a young, tender bear, serve it with a superior red wine. A good vintage Gamay or Pinot Noir is perfect. We would choose French Burgundy, one of the heavier lables. French bread, brandied carrots, and German potato casserole make this meal a delight.

MARINATED BEAR ROAST

Marinating wild game always has excellent results. Marinades have an acidic base, and this helps tenderize it. This is a simple recipe, but rather festive....Gather the following:

- **1 bear roast, preferably the tenderloin.**
- **1 cup dry red wine**
- **½ cup oil**
- **1 sliced carrot**
- **1 garlic clove, crushed (optional)**
- **1 teaspoon salt**
- **6 peppercorns**
- **1 bay leaf**

If the roast is from a hind quarter, it usually has a thick layer of fat. Trim this to a quarter-inch thickness. If you have stripped the tenderloin, ideal for this recipe, lard it with a larding needle with strips of beef suet.

Next, in a bowl, add a cup of dry red wine, half cup of oil, sliced carrot, garlic clove, salt, peppercorns, and a bay leaf. If the roast is large, you may have to double the recipe. Put the roast in the bowl and marinate for one to two days. Turn piece of meat occasionally.

When ready for the feast, preheat oven to 325°, and cook for 35 minutes per pound, or until the meat thermometer registers 170°. Serve with French bread, brandied carrots, and German potato casserole. A bottle of excellent heavy Burgundy makes this a magnificent meal.

BEAR FAT

There is no need to throw bear fat away. Save it to render. Once, reading a cook book published in the early 1800s, we noticed the author was adamant about the superiority of bear fat for pie crust. Black bear fat renders to a white consistency like lard.

BEAR CHOPS

Trim excess fat from the outside of the chop, and get ready for a recipe that has to be the simplest of all time. Put a tablespoon of oil in a cast-iron frying pan, and rub it around with your hand, making a coating. Put this pan on a medium-high heat. Lightly pepper the chops. When the pan begins to smoke a little, add the chops, quickly searing one side. With a spatula so you do not pierce the meat, turn carefully and brown the other side. Reduce heat to medium-low. This initial braising should not have taken more than five minutes. If the chops are an inch thick, cook 12 minutes, and then turn them. Cook another 12 minutes. They should be done. The ideal is to remove them as soon as the flesh in the center against the bone has turned from pink to brown, yet is still moist. Serve with a Bordeaux wine, mashed potatoes, mashed squash, and broccoli. Homemade rye bread will make the whole thing memorable. And, for an extra touch, before serving, put a thick pad of butter on each chop. Make sure there are enough chops for second helpings.

GERMAN POTATO CASSEROLE

This dish is sinfully delicious! Boil four potatoes, and allow to cool. When cold, peel and grate them. Then, gather the following ingredients:

    4 cooked, grated potatoes
    ¼ cup butter
    1 cup sour cream
    1 cup grated Cheddar cheese
    1 onion, grated
    salt and pepper to taste
    paprika

In a saucepan, melt the grated cheese and butter together. Add sour cream, grated onion, salt, and pepper, and blend thoroughly. Add the cooked, grated potatoes, and mix well. Add this to a buttered casserole dish. Sprinkle with paprika and bake for a half hour at 350°. Goes well with red-meat dishes.

BRANDIED CARROTS

This dish goes superbly with red meat. Carrots this month are as fresh and good as they ever get. You will need a quart of thinly sliced carrots. This is a simple recipe. Gather the following ingredients:

    1 quart thinly sliced carrots
    ⅓ cup water
    ¼ cup of sugar, or honey (we prefer honey!)
    ¼ cup brandy
    1 teaspoon salt

In a buttered casserole dish, put the thinly sliced carrots. Pour ⅓ cup of water over carrots. Then, a ¼ cup sugar or honey. Next, sprinkle on salt, then pour on ¼ cup brandy. Cover tightly, and cook in a preheated 350° oven for one hour, or until tender.

BRANDIED WILD CARROTS

This is an interesting variation of the above recipe. Instead of using domestic carrots, use wild carrots. Most everyone knows this plant, but most call it Queen Anne's Lace. The root of this flower is white like a parsnip, but very "carroty." Gather a quart of thinly sliced wild carrots, and use the above recipe.

MARINATED MOOSE STEAK

If you have some steak that is tough, make a marinade exactly as in the *Marinated Bear Roast* recipe, and marinated the steaks for one to two full days, turning them occasionally in the marinade. Cook the steaks on grill five inches from medium-dark coals, or under an oven broiler. Cooking time depends on the thickness of the steak. A one-inch piece takes from 20–25 minutes to cook to medium.

MOOSE STEW

An ideal supper for folks who have spent a day in the woods or on water. Use the *Venison Stew* recipe in the December chapter. Serve with hot biscuits or popovers, and coffee.

LAZY MAN'S MOOSE POT ROAST

If you suspect a roast is going to be tough, use this recipe. Prepare it exactly like the *Lazy Man's Venison Pot Roast* in the March chapter.

BEER MOOSE POT ROAST CANADIAN-STYLE

Chunk up some tough cuts of moose meat, and prepare exactly like the *Beer Venison Pot Roast Canadian-Style* in the March chapter.

A moose feeds on water plants, getting ready for a long winter. Photo courtesy of Maine Department of Inland Fisheries and Wildlife.

PAN-FRIED MOOSE STEAK

Moose is a true, epicurean delight. Few people who try this wonderful food dislike the flavor. It is less gamey than venison, and unlike bear, may be served rare, so it can truly be appreciated. Whether it is a wild meat or a filet mignon, well-done meat has a strike against it.

This recipe is simplicity in itself. All you need are tender moose steaks, clarified butter, pepper, and salt. First, sprinkle salt on one side of the steak, and pound it into the meat. If you are hygenically minded, use a wooden mallet. Otherwise, the hand works fine just slapping the meat. Turn it over, and do the same on the other side. We know salt is a "no-no" on meat before cooking, but there is a reason for our method. Pepper steaks lightly.

Next, melt a half-stick of butter in a frying pan, and clarify it. Heat clarified butter over a medium heat, and add steaks. The salt draws the butter into the meat, flavoring it wonderfully. The medium heat helps the process because the meat does not sear quickly. Serve with a Cabernet Sauvignon, German potato casserole, winter squash mashed, and a green veggie for color.

MOOSE ROAST

We know of a grammar school in Central Maine where a game warden occasionally gave the cooks moose meat he had confiscated. The cooks served it as roast beef, and we know the children never realized it was anything other than roast beef. Truly.

You need a tender cut for roasting. Whether it is beef, moose, bear, or venison, a good roast begins with a tender cut from a tender animal. Moose is lean, and really should have strips of beef suet drawn through it with a larding needle. If you do not have one, lay strips on roast and pin with toothpicks. Put pepper and garlic powder on the roast, lay it in a shallow baking dish on a rack, and bake in a preheated 325° oven. Use a meat thermometer for perfect results. Otherwise, cook 25 minutes per pound for a rare roast, or 30 minutes per pound for a medium roast. Serve with a great red wine, French bread, baked potatoes, mashed winter squash and a green veggie. Also, you might want Yorkshire pudding.

MARINATED MOOSE ROAST

If you suspect the roast is tough, prepare it in exactly the same manner as the *Marinated Bear Roast*. The results just might be astounding.

MOOSE KABOBS

This is an excellent time of year to make kabobs. Green peppers, tomatoes, and onion are fresh from your garden, and the mushrooms are fresh from the fields or forests. Moose, venison, lamb, or beef may be used. The meal is festive. An ideal epicurean delight to serve when good friends are over for dinner. First, gather the following ingredients for a marinade:

- **1 cup white wine**
- **½ cup oil**
- **juice from one lemon**
- **1 thinly sliced carrot**
- **1 garlic clove, crushed**
- **1 teaspoon salt**
- **6 peppercorns**
- **1 bay leaf**

Mix these ingredients in a large bowl. For each serving, you will need ¾ pound of meat cut into one-to-one-and-a-half-inch cubes. Select the tenderest cut of meat, and cube. Put this in the bowl with the marinade, and set in refrigerator for at least 12 hours. Before cooking, gather the following ingredients:

- **2 green peppers**
- **3 tomatoes**
- **3 medium onions**
- **1 pound of mushrooms**

Seed the peppers and cut into one-inch squares. Quarter the tomatoes. If they are large tomatoes, cut them into sixths. Quarter the onions. If you are using meadow mushrooms, they are too large to broil whole, so quarter them also. If they are small, commercial mushrooms, broil whole.

A lot of fine folks put chunks of meat on the skewer, alternating it with pieces of green pepper, tomatoes, onions, and mushrooms. It looks very festive, but we do not do it this way. When the meat is done, sometimes too well, the veggies are still raw. We skewer the vegetables first, brush them with a marinade that the meat has set in, then put them five inches from medium-dark coals. It may take as long as 15 minutes to cook these vegetables, depending on the heat of the coals. Five or six minutes before you feel the vegetables will be done, add meat, all clumped together for a rare shish kabob, or spaced apart a little for brown, crisp pieces. Brown the meat on all sides by turning the skewer. It won't take long with these cubes. Not more than a matter of minutes. Serve with corn-on-the-cob, French bread, and a Bordeaux wine. A real crowd pleaser that is easy for the host, freeing him or her to socialize. This meal could become a September tradition at your place.

GRILLED TOMATOES

Let's face it. If it has been a good tomato year, and you get carried away, as we do, and have put out 30 tomato plants—just in case it will be a bad tomato year—you will have tomatoes coming from your ears. This is a good way to deal with them. Simply cut them in half, and lay face down on medium-dark coals; 10 minutes later, carefully flip over and set on the grill with the face up. When tender and bubbling, serve. Watch your mouth! Hot tomatoes are hotter than anything. They go with almost anything....

PERFECT MASHED SQUASH

We have two secrets to good squash. First, we cook chunks of hubbard with chunks of acorn, butternut, or buttercup. The hubbards are wet squash, where the latter are dry. Blending two kinds makes a light, fluffy squash neither wet nor dry. This is one of those little differences family members appreciate. Second, we dry the squash just like potatoes in the Thomas Jefferson Boiled Potato recipe in the July chapter.

First, chunk up a peeled squash. Next, heat a third of a pot of water to a rapid boil. Have a teaspoon of salt in the water. Put the chunks in, and when the water boils again, reduce heat to medium-low. In about 20 minutes, the chunks should be tender enough to mash. Drain the water, put the pot back on the stove to dry the pieces, and shake so squash won't stick. In two or three minutes, remove from heat. For approximately four cups of mashed squash, add a quarter stick of butter. Dribble in just enough warm milk to get a fluffy consistency. Mash and whip until smooth and creamy. Plan on about half-a-cup per serving. Squash goes with nearly anything.

BAKED SQUASH

We love it! Truly. Baked squash is an American tradition. We like acorn, buttternut, or buttercup for baking. Just a personal preference. For Thanksgiving, we always bake green hubbard, but this is just a family tradition handed down through generations. We love the little species of squash better.

Slice a squash in half. You need a half squash for each serving. If that seems a little too much, quarter the squash after cooking. Scoop out the seeds, lay face down on a baking sheet, and put into a 325° oven for 40 minutes. Remove, turn the pieces over, baste heavily with butter, the more the merrier, and season with salt and pepper. Some people like to sprinkle brown sugar on at this time. We don't. Fresh squash is sweet enough. It goes famously with red meats, particularly roasts, Yorkshire pudding, rice pilaf, and a green veggie. Of course, a bottle of wine.

MARINATED MUSHROOMS

Marinated mushrooms make a grand appetizer. The recipe is simple, and a good way to use all of those meadow mushrooms during a good mushroom year. Gather the following ingredients:

- 1 **pound fresh, sliced mushrooms**
- ⅔ **cups of vinegar**
- 1½ **cups oil, preferably olive**
- 1 **teaspoon sugar**
- 2 **cloves garlic, crushed**
- 2 **medium onions, sliced and ringed**
  salt and pepper to taste

Mix the vinegar, oil, sugar, garlic, onion rings, salt, and pepper. In a bowl or jar, cover the mushrooms with this mixture, cover the bowl or jar, and refrigerate for at least eight hours.

Home-grown squash . . . many winter meals.   Ken Allen photo.

BAKED STUFFED MUSHROOMS

For baked stuffed mushrooms, you need large mushrooms with caps sizeable enough to fill. Finding these in supermarkets is a problem. If you are fortunate, try this recipe.

In September, a large species of mushroom grows in pastures, particularly where horses are present. We call them meadow mushrooms, and relish their fine flavor. Sometimes, we have picked them so easily we could fill grocery bags. In dry years, they are scarce. Gather the following:

- 4 mushrooms per person
- stems from each mushroom, finely chopped
- equal amount of cooked white-fleshed fish, chicken, salmon, crayfish, or crabmeat as there are stems, chopped finely
- 4 tablespoons butter
- 1 tablespoon grated onion
- ½ teaspoon salt
- ¼ teaspoon pepper
- 1 egg for each cup of combined mushroom stems and meat
- buttered bread crumbs for topping

Over a medium-low heat, melt four tablespoons of butter. Carefully remove the stems from the mushroom caps, and chop them finely. Sauté in butter until tender. Remove from heat. Brush the caps with the melted butter in pan, then put the mushroom stems and remaining butter in a mixing bowl. Add fish, chicken, salmon, crayfish, or crabmeat (we like the latter two) to the sautéed stems. The meat is chopped finely, and is the same amount as the mushroom stems. Add the onion, salt, and pepper, and mix thoroughly. For each cup of combined mushrooms and meat filling, add one beaten egg. Mix well. Lay mushroom caps, gill side up, on a buttered baking sheet. Heap the filling on, sprinkle on bread crumbs, and lay on butter. Bake in a preheated 350° oven for 15–20 minutes, or until mushrooms are tender and browned. A great appetizer. Serve with a bottle of Graves or Sauvignon Blanc.

WILD RICE

Wild rice has always been a favorite with game dishes. Nowadays, the price of it makes wild rice a luxury. However, wild rice, a tall, plume-topped grass, is found in shallow lakes and swamps around the Northeast. It is easy to recognize; yet, is difficult to harvest. You must work at it. The grain ripens in late summer and early fall, and must be watched closely. When it is too green, it won't thresh out. Two or three days later, the grain will shatter during the threshing. But, with a little experience and work, you can gather this wild food at the right time.

For harvesting, merely pole or paddle a canoe through a rice marsh. Have an oil cloth or piece of plastic lying on the canoe bottom. Tip the head of the rice plant over the canoe, and strike it sharply with a stick. Rice will fall onto the oil cloth or plastic. Collect just a little and take it home. Spread the seeds in a warm, sunny place to dry, then put it in a shallow baking pan in a preheated oven. Parch the grain, stirring it occasionally so it won't burn. It takes about an hour. Cool, then remove the husk off each kernel by rubbing briskly with your hands. Store the finished product in air-tight containers.

When you know the rice is ripe, return for a day, and gather all you can. Then, the real work begins. You realize why the price hovers around $15 a pound.

WILD RICE WITH BROWN RICE

Domestic rice is bland, so just three tablespoons of wild rice mixed with a cup of brown, and cooked together, gives the flavor of wild rice for much less the cost. We find ourselves eating this combination almost exclusively unless we have special guests, or a special occasion. Always rinse wild rice once before cooking to remove that disagreeable smoky taste.

WILD RICE

The nutty, somewhat smoky flavor of wild rice enhances a game dinner like nothing else. It is cooked in much the same manner as domestic rice, except you use more liquid. In a saucepan, bring three cups of water and a teaspoon of salt to a boil. While it heats, rinse a cup of wild rice in cold water; otherwise, it will have a disagreeably smoky flavor. One rinsing is adequate. Slowly stir the rice into boiling water. Cover saucepan tightly. When it boils again, reduce to low, and cook uncovered for 30 minutes, or until it is tender. Put in a buttered casserole dish, and put into a 325° preheated oven for 10–15 minutes. Have the rice dotted with butter, and the casserole dish tightly covered. This makes the rice fluffier.... Serve with wild game and superior red wines. Wild rice is one of the world's great luxury foods.

We hate to see September go. It is a marvelous month to eat, drink, and revel in the bounties of the season. But, the glories of October are close by, and that month can make us forget anything....

Chapter 11
October

October. Nature's explosion of colors. Fall foliage under high, blue skies, higher than they ever get, and crisp, sun-splashed days. Even rainy Monday mornings have charm. The year at its finest.

Our idea of heaven would be eternal October. Falling leaves and flying footballs. Apple presses and country roads. Golden stalks of corn and piles of pumpkins. And smoothbores and bird dogs. Not any smoothbore or bird dog. But yours. Your fowling piece with the blueing well-worn, and a dog with your soul in its eyes. All against a backdrop of color. A vagrant's month. Pure and simple.

A grand season for cookery. Maybe the best. Grouse land in the family larder, and if God created a finer food, we have yet to see it. Roasted grouse is a dish rich in tradition and romance.

ROASTED GROUSE

Did you ever hear anyone say grouse is too dry for his or her palate? This is a constant reminder to us that this bird is a challenge in the kitchen. It is easy to ruin! Properly cooked, it is a moist, succulent food that has just a subtle game taste. If bear and moose epitomize primeval wilderness, grouse embodies hedges, field edges, and friendly stream bottoms close to civilization.

Properly prepared grouse begins shortly after a string of pellets intercepts one in flight. As soon as you are out of the cover, eviscerate immediately, and if there is a wild apple tree handy, quarter an apple and stuff it in the cavity. At home, after the bird has cooled, pluck carefully, taking care not to tear the skin. Some folks skin grouse. This certainly does not help keep the bird moist during cooking. After plucking, clean the cavity carefully with a damp cloth, then make a bread stuffing.

Poultry Bread Stuffing

Gather the following ingredients:

- 2 tablespoons butter
- 2 medium onions, chopped coarsely
- 2 celery stalks, thinly sliced
- 6 slices dry bread
- 1 lightly beaten egg
- 1 teaspoon poultry seasoning
- 1 diced, boiled potato
- ¼ teaspoon garlic powder
- enough milk to moisten stuffing
- salt and pepper to taste

Chop two onions and slice two stalks of celery, and sauté over a medium-low heat until onions begin to turn translucent. Remove from heat. Crumble six slices of dry bread, then add melted butter, onions, and celery. Add one lightly beaten egg, teaspoon of poultry seasoning, diced potato, garlic powder, salt, and pepper. Mix thoroughly. We like the potato because it makes a moister stuffing. Add milk, just a little at a time. When the stuffing is moist enough for your taste, let it stand for 15 minutes. This improves the flavor.

Lightly stuff, then truss one bird for each two people. Lay the birds in a shallow baking dish that has been liberally smeared with butter. Sprinkle paprika on the birds for color. Next, and we hate to admit this, we resort to aluminum foil. This is one of the few recipes where we use foil. We cover the birds, and lightly tuck the foil under. The grouse go into a preheated 300° oven for two hours. This covering plus the slow cooking keeps the meat moist. At the end of two hours, place the birds under a broiler, and brown. This only takes two or three minutes.

Serve with French bread, baked-stuffed tomatoes, a green veggie, and a great French Chablis. Our favorite meal of the entire season. Truly....

PLUM WINE GROUSE

This recipe is superb for yearling birds. It is a recipe originally used with Cornish hens, a good substitute if you are not a grouse hunter. Gather the following:

- 2 **grouse (or Cornish hens)**
- 4 **tablespoons butter**
- ¼ **cup of plum wine, or medium sherry**
- 2 **tablespoons lemon juice**
- 1 **teaspoon dry mustard**
- 2 **teaspoons soy sauce**
  poultry bread stuffing (optional)

Stuff and truss birds, and place in a shallow baking dish. Melt four tablespoons butter, and mix in a quarter cup of plum wine, two tablespoons lemon juice, a teaspoon of dry mustard, and two teaspoons soy sauce. Mix thoroughly. Baste birds with this sauce, letting excess drip into pan. Place the birds in a preheated 375° oven, and cook for approximately 35 minutes. During the cooking, baste quickly every five minutes, glazing the birds well. When done, the leg joints will move easily. Don't overcook and dry them out. Serve with French bread, rice pilaf, baked squash, a green veggie, and a good bottle of Chablis.

A grouse for the family larder. More than a memory . . . but the makings of a meal fit for kings and lesser royalty.   Ken Allen photo.

EUSTIS GROUSE

For want of another name, we call this Eustis Grouse. We could say Grouse au vin, fricasseed grouse, or wine grouse, but none quite fit the simplicity of the dish.

One wet day in the Eustus area, when the weather was unable to decide whether to rain or snow, so was doing a little of both, we cooked two grouse on a Coleman stove on our pick-up's tailgate. It was a spur-of-the-moment meal, and all we had to work with were butter, salt, pepper, poultry seasoning, and wine. Gather the following:

- 1 **stick of butter**
- ½ **cup wine**
- ½ **teaspoon salt**
- ¼ **teaspoon pepper**
- 1–2 **teaspoons poultry seasoning**

In a cast-iron frying pan, clarify a stick of butter over a medium-low heat. Turn to medium, then prepare the serving pieces of grouse. First, pat them dry, sprinkle with pepper and poultry seasoning, and brown quickly in the clarified butter. Add wine and salt, and as soon as it bubbles, reduce heat to low, cover tightly, and simmer for 45-60 minutes. If you are under a sky high, wide, and blue, you'll need nothing else to feel like royalty. Even on a miserable day, we felt like royalty.

COLD ROAST GROUSE

Use the Roasted Grouse recipe with a slight variation. Since the end result is an October picnic, the stuffing recipe will have no dairy products in it, hoping to eliminate the problem of food poisoning from day-old bird stuffing. Substitute margarine for butter, water for milk, and leave out the egg. Serve this bird with French bread, cold mashed potato salad, chilled, boiled eggs, cheeses, and fruits. An excellent bottle of Chablis rounds this meal out.

SAUTÉED WOODCOCK

Austere simplicity. Take two woodcock for each serving, and split them down the back with poultry sheers. On the side board, spread the bird out, breast-side up. Press down hard with the palm, and flatten the bird. Really squash it. Season lightly with pepper. In a cast-iron frying pan, melt four tablespoons of butter over a medium heat. Lay the birds in the pan breast down, and brown. Turn and brown other side. To fully appreciate this gourmet delight, serve medium-rare to medium. Serve with wild rice, baked squash, French bread, and a good red wine. We would appreciate a French Burgundy, or at least, Cabernet Sauvignon. You need a green vegetable for color, so why not have Brussels sprouts, hopefully from your garden.

MEDALLION OF WOODCOCK

If you and close friends have really gotten into a fall of woodcock, and have a great day's shooting, try this recipe just once. Filet the breast of each woodcock. You will get a small, medallion-shaped filet from each side of a breast. Lightly pepper, and sauté in melted butter. Serve this as an appetizer with a bottle of Bordeaux wine. Surprisingly, this tastes similar to venison cooked in butter. Truly.

Save the woodcock bodies, and make a soup as an appetizer for the following evening. Make it just like beef-barley soup. Nothing from the wild should be wasted.

WOODCOCK BAKED IN CREAM

Another simple recipe. You need two woodcock per serving. The birds should be plucked, leaving the skin intact. This is important for baking. Put an onion wedge in each cavity, skewer shut, then rub the outside of the bird with soft butter. Lightly pepper. Lay birds on a buttered baking pan, baste with heavy cream, and put into a 375° preheated oven. You don't need much cream. Not more than a tablespoon or two per bird. Baste birds every five minutes with the cream and juices in the baking pan. Cook until the woodcock are brown, and serve medium-rare to medium. It should not take more than 20–30 minutes. Serve with wild rice, baked squash, a green vegetable, French bread, and a good red wine.

BACON WOODCOCK

Bacon has a strong flavor, but it is difficult to overpower woodcock—quite rich in flavor. You need two plucked woodcocks per person. Put an onion wedge in each cavity, and skewer shut. Lay woodcock on a greased baking pan, and wrap a thin piece of bacon around each breast. Season with pepper, and put into a 450° preheated oven until the bacon is browned. This should take no more than 12 or so minutes. Serve with rice pilaf, baked squash, Brussels sprouts, French bread, and a good dry red wine.

ROASTED PHEASANT

Use the same recipe as the *Roasted Grouse*. Pheasant tends to be dry also. The Poultry Bread Stuffing will make some gourmets shudder. Bread stuffing is supposed to pick up the gamey taste of wild animals. With grouse, pheasant, and even woodcock, this is no problem, particularly with the extra dosage of onions in our stuffing. Roasted pheasant is a delight that calls for rice pilaf, French bread, and a white wine.

LARDED, ROASTED PHEASANT

This is a superior recipe for pheasant. Take a carefully plucked bird, rub soft butter on it, pepper lightly, then put a Poultry Bread Stuffing or a quartered onion in the cavity. Skewer it shut. Lay on a greased baking sheet, and liberally cover the body with strips of fresh pork fat—not salt pork. Bake in 325° preheated oven for 30 minutes per pound.

FRICASSEED PHEASANT

Fricasseeing is an excellent way to prepare an old pheasant you suspect is tougher than a hemlock knot. Gather the following ingredients:

- 2 pheasants, cut into serving pieces
- 1 cup flour
- 1 teaspoon salt
- 1 teaspoon poultry seasoning
- ½ teaspoon oregano
- ½ teaspoon pepper
- ¼ heaping teaspoon garlic powder
- 4 tablespoons oil or clarified butter

Put one cup flour, teaspoon salt, teaspoon poultry seasoning, half-teaspoon oregano, and quarter-teaspoon pepper in a paper bag, and shake to mix ingredients. Put the oil or clarified butter in a Dutch oven, and place on a medium-high heat. As this heats, drop the pieces of pheasant into the paper bag two or three at a time, and shake bag, covering pieces with dry mixture. When the oil is good and hot, slip the floured pieces into the oil, and brown quickly on both sides. This may have to be done in two or three steps if you have large pieces of pheasant from big birds. After the pieces have been browned, reduce the heat to low, barely cover the pieces with water, add the heaping ¼ teaspoon of garlic powder, and simmer for two to three hours. The flour on the pheasant will thicken this gravy a little. Serve with buttered noodles, a green vegetable, biscuits, and tea or coffee.

PHEASANT AU VIN

This is merely coq au vin, with a pheasant substitute. It sounds fancy, but it's not. Just darn fine eating and simple to make. It is ideal for tough birds because there is a long cooking time in a wine broth.

First, cut two pheasant into serving pieces, and save the neck, wing tips, giblets, and stray pieces of skin for a broth. Then, gather the following ingredients:

2 pheasants, cut into serving pieces
necks, wing tips, giblets, etc. for broth
½ teaspoon salt
1 teaspoon poultry seasoning
1 teaspoon celery seeds (optional)
2½ cups water

Put the necks, wing tips, giblets, and stray pieces of pheasant skin in a pot. Add salt, poultry seasoning, and water. Celery seeds are optional; however, if you have never used celery seeds for soups, buy some. You will not regret it. Bring the liquid to a boil, reduce heat to low, and simmer for an hour. In the end, you will need two cups of broth.

While this simmers, gather the following ingredients, and start the pheasant.

1 cup flour
1 teaspoon salt
¼ heaping teaspoon pepper
1 heaping teaspoon poultry seasoning
¼ teaspoon garlic powder
4 tablespoons of oil
1 tablespoon of butter
1 pound button mushrooms
1 pound small, whole onions
2 cups of broth
2 cups of red wine

Put flour, salt, pepper, poultry seasoning, and garlic powder in a paper bag, and shake, mixing the ingredients. Next, put two tablespoons of oil and a half-tablespoon of butter in a cast-iron frying pan, then do the same with another frying pan. Put them on a medium heat. While these heat, drop pheasant pieces into the paper bag, and shake, coating pieces thoroughly. Slip pieces into frying pans and brown well. Don't crowd the pheasant pieces. The pieces will not be entirely cooked, but don't worry. Put the pieces in one large casserole dish, or two smaller ones. Add the pound of button mushrooms. These should be sautéed to a light tan. Also, add the pound of small, whole onions. Put the two cups of broth over the pheasant, then two cups of red wine. Bake in a preheated 275° oven for one-and-a-half-to-two hours. The results is a simply prepared meal that looks elegant. The wine and slow cooking will tenderize the toughest bird, but the real beauty of this meal is in the preparation. You can prepare it in the afternoon, and reheat it at dinner time, freeing you for other chores, or pleasures. Rice pilaf, French bread, Brussels sprouts, baked squash, and a Cabernet Sauvignon accompany this meal beautifully.

PHEASANT IN SOUR CREAM

A festive meal. It is a good way to treat a tough bird. Gather the following ingredients:

- 1 pheasant, cut into serving pieces
- ½ cup flour
- 1 teaspoon salt
- ¼ teaspoon pepper
- 1 teaspoon paprika (optional)
- 4 tablespoons oil
- 3 tablespoons butter
- 1 cup broth, or water
- ½ teaspoon thyme (optional)
- ¼ cup brandy (optional)
- 1 cup sour cream
- ½ teaspoon celery seed

Cut a pheasant into serving pieces, saving wing tips, neck, giblets, and stray pieces of skin. Set the serving pieces aside. Put the rest in a saucepan, then add one-and-a-quarter cups of water, salt, pepper, pinch of garlic powder, and half teaspoon celery seeds. Simmer for one hour. You will need a cup of this broth for the recipe.

Put the flour, salt, pepper, and paprika in a paper bag, and shake to mix. Put the four tablespoons of oil and three tablespoons of butter in a cast-iron frying pan, and set on a medium-high heat. While it heats, drop the pheasant pieces into the bag, shake, and coat the pieces thoroughly. Slip the pieces into the hot fat, and brown on all sides quickly. Remove the pieces as soon as browned. Dump off all but one tablespoon of cooking fat and put back on stove at medium-high heat. There will be brown crusting on the pan's bottom. Dump a cup of broth into the pan. It should really make quite a noise on the medium-high heat. Scrape the pan's bottom, removing the brown crusting. Stir the broth until smooth. During this stirring, add the thyme and a quarter-cup of brandy. Brandy is optional, but makes a delightful difference.

Lower the heat to low, lay the pheasant pieces into the pan, and simmer until tender. This may only take 45 minutes with a yearling bird; an hour-and-a-half with an old breeder cock. During cooking, occasionally wiggle a leg joint, or press a wooden spoon gently against the breast. As the bird becomes tender, you get the feel. When done, add the sour cream. When it begins to bubble, serve with buttered egg noodles, broccoli, rye bread, and Cabernet Sauvignon or a great Bordeaux. This meal makes you feel like royalty.

PHEASANT IN CREAM

Use the above Pheasant in Sour Cream recipe, but when you get to the part where you add the cup of broth, just add a half cup. Scrape the pan's bottom, and stir. Add brandy and thyme, and stir. Put the pheasant pieces into a casserole dish and dump the brandy and broth mixture over it. Add a cup of heavy cream, and bake in a 325° preheated oven for one hour and 15 minutes. Serve with buttered egg noodles, broccoli, rye bread, and a good red wine. It may become a family tradition.

The stuff dreams are made of. A youngster's success and the making of an elegant meal later. Photo courtesy of Maine Department of Inland Fisheries and Wildlife.

FRIED SQUIRREL

America grew up, eating squirrels. When majestic mast trees stretched from Georgia to New England, squirrels thrived on abundant mast crops. Squirrels were there all right. Willing targets for pioneers with sharp eyes and long rifles.

As children, we ate a lot of fried squirrels, and loved their nutty, subtle gamey flavor. This recipe seems to be the only way anyone prepared them. This recipe is austere simplicity. Gather the following ingredients:

- **2–4 squirrels, cut into serving pieces**
- **salt and pepper to taste**
- **½ cup water**

Soak the pieces of squirrel in salted water. Just lay the pieces in a bowl, cover with water, and add a teaspoon of salt. Let sit in a refrigerator for an hour. You may want to change the water if it becomes too red. Remove pieces, and pat dry. Put oil into a cast-iron frying pan, adding just enough to thoroughly cover bottom. Place on a medium-high heat. When it gets hot, lightly salt and pepper the pieces, and add to the oil. Brown quickly on both sides. Add a half cup of water, and simmer until meat is tender. It may take an hour-and-a-half, so make sure heat is on low, and the pan is tightly covered. Serve with Southern Fried Potatoes, biscuits, and lots of coffee or tea.

SQUIRREL STEW

America certainly grew up on squirrel stew. Use the recipe in Chapter 2 for *Rabbit Stew*.

SQUIRREL PIE

It is difficult not to be a glutton with meat pies. Use the recipe in Chapter 2 for *Rabbit Pie*.

FRICASSEED SQUIRREL

This recipe is ideal for the toughest old squirrel. Use the *Fricasseed Rabbit* recipe from Chapter 2.

SQUIRREL OVER NOODLES

This elevates squirrel to festive proportions. It is a good recipe, especially effective for older members of a squirrel clan. Use the recipe from Chapter 3 for Rabbit over Noodles.

CAMP-STYLE SQUIRREL

This is an excellent recipe. Bacon is used, and this flavor always pleases the most finicky of palates. Gather the following ingredients:

- 2–4 squirrels, cut into serving pieces
- 8 slices of bacon
- 1 large onion, chopped coarsely
- ½ pound mushrooms (optional)
- 1 teaspoon salt
- ¼ teaspoon pepper
- 2–3 tablespoons clarified butter or oil
- ¼ cup brandy

You need two cast-iron frying pans for this dish. Put two to three tablespoons of clarified butter or oil in a frying pan, and put it aside. Next, in a cold frying pan, lay eight strips of bacon, and cook until they just turn crisp. Remove bacon, and dump out all but two or three tablespoons of fat. Add the mushrooms. You may chop or slice them. Whole mushrooms would be all right. This a democratic dish. Also, add the chopped onions. Put the heat on medium-low. When the onions just begin to turn brown, remove pan from heat.

Take the squirrel pieces that have been soaked for at least an hour in salted water, and pat them dry. Over a medium-high heat, brown them quickly in two to three tablespoons of clarified butter or oil. While still sizzling, add salt, pepper, and brandy. Reduce heat to low. You also may want to remove the pan to cool for a minute or two. Add the bacon strips, crumbled, and sautéed mushrooms, onions, and bacon drippings used for the sautéing. Cover tightly, and simmer for at least an hour. Serve with biscuits, Southern Fried Potatoes, and string beans.

Hardwood split into kindling-size pieces burns quickly to coals. (Ken Allen photo)

BAKED STUFFED TOMATOES

This time of year, folks with gardens should have tomatoes coming from their ears. The following recipe is a great change of pace for tomatoes, and goes with grouse or pheasant like peaches and cream. This recipe may start a family tradition. Gather the following ingredients:

- 4 large, ripe tomatoes
- 1 cup uncooked rice
- 2 tablespoons oil
- 1 clove garlic, crushed
- 1 onion, chopped
- 2 cups water, or chicken broth
- 2 bouillon cubes, if you use water
- parsley
- 1 teaspoon salt
- ¼ teaspoon pepper
- ½ teaspoon marjoram (optional)
- dry bread crumbs to cover each tomato
- ¼ pound grated cheese

In a Dutch oven, preferably cast-iron (it does a superior job with rice), add two tablespoons of oil. Go light with the oil. Too much makes rice taste greasy. Set oven on a medium heat. Add the chopped onion and crushed garlic clove. Don't sauté the garlic clove more than two to three minutes. It will kill the clove's flavor. At the end of two to three minutes, remove the clove. Sauté the onions until they just begin to turn brown, then add the uncooked rice, and stir, coating each grain with oil.

Have a saucepan with two cups of chicken broth or two cups of water with dissolved bouillon cubes boiling. Add this to the Dutch oven. Within seconds, the liquid should boil again. Add salt, pepper, and marjoram and stir quickly, but gently. Reduce the heat to low and cook five minutes uncovered. Cover tightly, and cook for 40 minutes without removing the cover. While the rice cooks, cut the tops from the tomatoes, and scoop out pulp from the center. Save pulp. When the rice has cooked for 40 minutes, lift the cover quickly, stir two or three times quickly but gently, and recover. Let it sit for 10 minutes. This makes rice fluffier. Add the tomato pulp, and stir. Stuff the tomatoes with this rice and tomato pulp mixture. Cover the tops with bread crumbs. Sprinkle on a generous amount of cheese, then bake in a shallow baking dish in a 300° preheated oven for one hour. When done, put a sprig of parsley or parsley flakes on each tomato, and serve with any delightful food. We love it....

Eat drink, and be merry. November with its rain, browns, and grays is but moments away. And, even if you are not a deer hunter, November has fine moments. A month tailored to a cook.

An early season bird cover. Photo courtesy of Maine Department of Inland Fisheries and Wildlife.

Chapter 12
November

November. Browns and grays, and so often, endless rain. It is the end of the road for another year. Foliage and fruit have died, and waterfowl and other migratory birds have gone south. Sunrises are bare and silent except for an occasional rattled bluejay.

Many folks dislike the month. Simply hate it. A pity. The month is to be appreciated. A time of essentials with no activities to confuse the mind. Just rattling limbs and long shadows. A season not a season. Rather, a suspension in time. A precious interlude between autumn's profusion of colors and winter's white. A time good for thinking. And eating.

OUR FAVORITE VENISON STEAK RECIPE

Venison is November's bounty. It needs no apologies. Cooked properly, venison is food fit for the Gods. This first recipe is directly from the French cooking school. In that corner of the world, beef is much leaner than in America, and special methods of cookery developed. Since venison is 40 percent leaner than U.S. beef, the following recipe is perfect.

First, take some deer steaks (or chops) and sprinkle with a liberal amount of salt. Cover one side, then pound the salt right into the meat. You may use your hand and slap it really hard onto the meat, or for the more hygenically minded, pound it in with a wooden spoon or mallet. Turn the meat over and do the same on the other side. Sprinkle on pepper to taste, then get the butter ready.

Over a medium heat, clarify a half stick of butter in a cast-iron frying pan. You may want to skim the foam two or three times, cooling the butter a little between each skimming. Save the foam to pour on the finished steak or chops.

Keep the heat on medium, and slide in the steaks. The salt draws the clarified butter into the meat, and the result is delightful. Cook to medium-rare, or medium at most, and serve with mashed potatoes, Brussels sprouts, home-made bread, and serve with a dry red wine. A Medoc would make the meal memorable.

BROILED VENISON STEAK

Broiling tends to dry venison. Try this simple recipe. Gather the following ingredients:

- 2 medium onions, chopped
- 1 tablespoon butter
- 2 tablespoons oil
- 1 teaspoon lemon juice
- ½ teaspoon salt
- ¼ teaspoon pepper

Place a small cast-iron frying pan over a medium-low heat, and add butter, oil, lemon juice, salt, and pepper. When the butter melts, mix everything thoroughly. As it begins to bubble, add the chopped onions and cook until they are translucent. Try not to brown the butter and, definitely, do not brown the onions.

Liberally brush the steaks with the butter-oil-lemon juice mixture, and place under a preheated 550° broiler. Leave the steaks under the broiler until the juices bead on top. Remove from the broiler and baste the uncooked side. Put back under the broiler, and cook the uncooked side until the juices bead on top again. By then, it should be medium-rare. Don't let the color on the outside of the meat fool you. The basting keeps it a pale-tan color, looking really uncooked. However, if you waited for this basted meat to char, the inside would be overcooked.

If you are cooking over coals, lightly baste one side of the steak, and lay the basted side down. If too much basting is on this side, it will just flare up when it drips onto the coals. Baste the top side lightly as it cooks. If the coals are medium heat (you should be able to hold your hand six inches away for five seconds), cook four to six minutes per side. When broiling meat over coals, it should be this medium heat for best results. Serve with creamy, mashed potatoes, a green veggie, tossed salad, homemade bread, and a good red Bordeaux wine.

BROILED VENISON CHOPS

Use the above recipe. Chops are a real delight. A favorite of ours.

VENISON ROAST

There are a couple of secrets to cooking venison roast. First, cook in a moderately slow oven around 300°. Certainly not more than 325°. The second secret is to draw several pieces of beef suet through the roast with a *larding needle*. If you have no larding needle, at least lay many strips of beef suet (or salt pork) on the roast. If you feel a need to secure the pieces, tie it with string. Don't use toothpicks or needles because the puncture holes allow precious juices to escape. Venison tends to be dry anyway.

Many folks are afraid to eat wild game unless it is well-done. This particularly does an injustice to venison roast. It should be served medium-rare, or medium at most. A meat thermometer will give perfect results, but if you have none, 25–30 minutes per pound should give you a medium-rare roast...at 300°.

If you have a young deer, preferably a yearling, you might want to roast a whole hind quarter—just like leg of lamb. Cook a hind quarter 30–35 minutes per pound at 325°. This should give you a medium roast.

Since deer fat tends to be tallowy, a rack in the roasting pan is a must to keep the roast above the fat. Tallow is the reason folks in pod auger days traditionally served hot tea with venison roast. The hot beverage rinses the tallow from your mouth. With a rack, tallow should be no problem.

Venison roast is an eloquent meal deserving the finest wine. Serve a French Burgundy, preferably a heavy Burgundy such as Chambertin or Nuits-Saint-Georges. French bread, asparagus, and Swedish Baked Potatoes make a meal dreams are made of.

SWEDISH BAKED POTATOES

This dish is certain to impress family and friends. You will need one medium to large potato for each serving. Peel each potato, then make paper thin slices across the width of the potato. *Do not slice all the way through the potato.* To keep from slipping and cutting the potato in half, lay it between two wooden spoons. The spoons will keep you from cutting all the way through. Make these papery thin slices across the potato from one end to the other. When cooking, these slices begin to spread out and brown on the edges to a festive, golden color.

Put in a 400° preheated oven and cook for one hour. Baste occasionally with melted butter that has chopped parsley and a touch of garlic in it. The result is delightful.

STUFFED VENISON ROAST

Use the venison roast recipe in this chapter. However, 45 minutes before the roast is done, remove the strips of fat, and cover the roast with a Poultry Bread Stuffing (Chapter 11). This browns nicely and makes a festive setting. Make sure the dressing is especially moist, even wet. It dries quickly on top of a meat rather than in a cavity. If it is too dry, the stuffing will absorb precious moisture from the roast.

Serve with a superior bottle of French Burgundy, asparagus, Swedish baked potatoes, and French bread. Enjoy.

Afternoons afield are the stuff dreams are made of . . . Ken Allen photo.

BREADED VENISON CUTLET

If you happen to get some venison from a yearling or a really tender deer, try this wonderful recipe. With a sharp knife, slice thin steaks not more than ⅜ of an inch thick. Lay them on a cutting board, then pound with the edge of a heavy saucer, breaking down all the fibers. This may take a little time, but the results are perfectly delightful.

Gather the following ingredients:

- **2 cutlets per serving**
- **1 cup flour**
- **2 cups bread crumbs**
- **salt and pepper to taste**
- **2 lightly beaten eggs**
- **4 tablespoons butter**
- **2 tablespoons oil**

Put the flour in a paper bag, eggs in a bowl, and bread crumbs in a pie plate. Salt and pepper the flour and bread crumbs to taste.

Put the butter and oil in a heavy cast-iron frying pan, and place on a medium heat. When it becomes hot, and begins to bubble, drop the cutlets into the bag of flour. Shake the bag, coating the pieces well. Shake excess flour from each piece, dip into the egg, then roll in bread crumbs. Sauté the cutlets on both sides until they are good and brown—about 10 minutes.

If you are unable to get each cutlet into the pan, do not bread them until there is space in the pan.

Serve this dish with creamy mashed potatoes, frenched string beans with slivered almonds, French bread, and a tossed salad. You may want to try something entirely different for a change-of-pace meal, so go Italian! Serve the breaded cutlets with spaghetti, tossed salad, home-made garlic bread, and a Chianti wine.

Venison is a fine meal . . . fit for royalty. It is also healthful. Photo courtesy of Maine Department of Inland Fisheries and Wildlife.

VENISON DIANE

An eloquent dish, simple to prepare, and guaranteed to impress family and friends. You will need thin, tender slices of steak for this dish. Gather the following:

- **8 thinly sliced steaks**
- **salt...enough to sprinkle on each one...both sides**
- **pepper to taste**
- **2 tablespoons butter**
- **1 medium onion, thinly sliced**
- **2 tablespoons brandy**
- **2 heaping tablespoons minced parsley**
- **1 tablespoon catsup or tomato sauce**
- **dash of Tabasco Sauce**
- **¼ cup dry red wine**

Lightly sprinkle salt on each piece of steak and pound it into the meat with your hand or a wooden mallet or spoon. Do each side of the steak. Then, sprinkle pepper on both sides, preferably freshly ground pepper.

Next, in a cast-iron frying pan, melt two tablespoons of butter over a medium heat. When the butter begins to bubble, sauté the steaks two minutes per side. Then, add the thinly sliced onion, and sauté one minute.

Now, the fancy part. Add two tablespoons of brandy and light it. Make sure there are no curtains or other flammables near the stove. When the brandy burns out on its own, add remaining ingredients and simmer until well blended. This should be no more than three or four minutes after it begins to bubble.

Pour the sauce equally over each steak, and serve with rice pilaf, Brussels sprouts, baked squash, French bread, and a good Cabernet Sauvignon. A memorable meal to make believers from non-venison eaters.

LIVER AND ONIONS

When we were young, deer liver, home fries, and eggs were a traditional hunter's breakfast. Slices of crisp bacon and fried onions rounded the morning feast out. Whatever time of day, deer liver is superior to pork, calf, or beef liver. Some folks simply love it, and live from year to year, hoping to add a deer liver to the family larder.

Bacon fat is traditional for cooking this dish, but shortening will do. First, gather the following ingredients:

- **2 tablespoons of bacon fat or shortening**
- **2 medium onions, chopped**
- **liver sliced to ½-inch thickness**
- **salt and pepper to taste**
- **1 cup flour**

Place a cast-iron frying pan over a medium heat, and add the shortening or bacon fat. When it begins to bubble, add the chopped onions. Then, mix the flour, salt, and pepper thoroughly. As the onions begin to turn translucent, dredge the liver in the flour, and add to the fry pan.

Some people like deer liver slightly pink, but if you must cook it thoroughly, make sure to remove it just as the inside turns from pink to brown. If it is cooked longer, it begins to resemble shoe leather.

Serve smothered with onions. If it is a breakfast dish, serve with homefries, bacon, eggs, and fried onions. For lunch or supper, creamy mashed potatoes, carrots, and biscuits are the thing. Coffee or tea should round the meal out.

VENISON BOURGUIGNON

This meal sounds snobbish, but is really simple to prepare. It is ideal to serve company. Not only is the dish eloquent, it may be made ahead, freeing you to prepare side dishes, or entertain.

This is really just a French stew traditionally made with beef. Venison makes an excellent substitute for beef. Since the recipe calls for marinating and then for long, slow cooking, it tenderizes all but the toughest cuts. Also, the salt-pork fat and butter for searing does not make a greasy meal with venison, a meat 40 percent leaner than an average cut of beef.

First, gather the following ingredients:

- **2 cups dry red wine**
- **1 bay leaf**
- **1 quartered onion, stuck with 2 cloves**
- **3 pounds of meat, cut in 2-inch cubes**

Put the cubed meat in a bowl, and add wine, bay leaf, and quartered onion with cloves. Marinate for 12–24 hours.

Next, gather the following ingredients when you are ready to put it together:

- ½ cup flour
- 1 teaspoon salt
- ½ teaspoon pepper
- 2 tablespoons butter
- ¼ cup diced salt pork
- 2 medium onions, chopped
- 1 garlic clove, minced
- ¼ cup brandy
- 1 cup beef broth
- 18 small, mushrooms
- 18 small, pearl onions
- minced parsley for garnish

Put the flour, salt, and pepper in a paper bag, and shake, mixing the ingredients. Next, put two tablespoons of butter in an oven-proof Dutch oven, and place on a medium heat. If you do not have an oven-proof Dutch oven, put aluminum foil on the handles before placing it in an oven.

After the butter melts and begins to sizzle, add the diced salt pork, and sauté quickly. When browned, remove the pieces. You may want to save them for garnish.

While the salt pork cooks, remove the meat from the marinade, saving the marinade for later. Pat the pieces of meat dry with a paper towel. Put the meat into the paper bag, and shake vigorously, coating the cubes well. After removing the salt pork, lay the meat in the Dutch oven, and brown on all sides quickly. While it browns, add chopped onions, and just two minutes before you are through browning the pieces, add the minced garlic clove.

Two minutes after adding the minced garlic clove, add the strained marinade, ¼ cup of brandy, and cup of beef broth. The pan will really sizzle. With a wooden spoon, scrape the bottom of the oven. Flour from the meat will have coated it. Scrape it all off, and stir until the broth is smooth.

Cover tightly, and place in a preheated 275° oven for 2½ to 3 hours. During the last hour, sauté the mushrooms until they are golden brown, but not overcooked. Add the mushrooms to the Venison Bourguignon. In the same skillet, add a teaspoon of sugar, and sauté the small onions. When nicely glazed, add to the Dutch oven also.

By now, if the gravy is not a rich brown, add a tablespoon of gravy coloring, but that is strictly optional. We seldom bother with it.

Serve this dish with buttered-parsleyed potatoes, Brussels sprouts, carrots, and French bread. These long, slender loaves are a must with this meal. Serve with Cabernet Sauvignon and feast. This is going to be a memorable meal.

VENISON HEART

When we were young, venison heart was served sliced cold in a sandwich. It is difficult to improve on this method.

In a saucepan, cover the heart with water, and add a teaspoon salt for each quart of water. Add a stalk of celery, a quartered onion, and pepper. Bring to a rapid boil, then reduce heat to simmer. Simmer the heart for two to three hours, tenderizing it. Let cool in a refrigerator.

With a sharp knife or slicer, slice the heart into paper-thin slices. Serve on home-made rye bread with mustard. Beer is great with this sandwich. Pickles and chips round it out.

PAN-BROILED VENISON

This is a simple recipe for chops or tender cuts of steak. Lightly smear butter onto the bottom of a cast-iron frying pan. This should be very light. Sprinkle salt into the pan, then place on a medium heat. Just a second before the butter begins to brown, add the steaks or chops, and sear quickly. Turn over, and sear the other side. Leave in the pan until the juices bead on top of the meat, then turn, and wait for the juices to bead again. It is ready to serve.

Creamy mashed potatoes, carrots, tossed salad, sautéed onions, mushrooms, and green peppers, and home-made rye bread dress up this simple dish. A good Bordeaux wine would make it memorable.

SAUTÉED MUSHROOMS, GREEN PEPPERS, AND ONIONS

This is a great side dish for any steak or chop recipe. It is a zesty combination that complements a simple meal, making it one of memory. Gather the following ingredients:

- 2–3 tablespoons of butter
- 1 cup mushrooms, sliced lengthwise
- 1 green pepper, sliced lengthwise, very thin
- 2 medium onions, thinly sliced
- pepper to taste
- touch of garlic powder in butter

Melt the butter in a cast-iron frying pan over a medium heat. Add the garlic powder and pepper. When the butter begins to bubble well, add the mushrooms, green peppers, and onions. When they begin to cook, stir occasionally, and sauté for eight minutes. Serve right from the pan sitting on the table.

Eat, drink, and smile at the moon. November is a month of memories, and a season for the thinking man. Certainly, a time to be appreciated...even with the sometimes endless rain.

Deer hunters on a tote road in the big woods. Photo courtesy of Maine Department of Inland Fisheries and Wildlife.

Chapter 13
December

December. The dark, festive month far from spring. Days of trout and fiddleheads, salmon and raspberries, upland fowl and wild rice, venison and wild mushrooms...all fresh...are over for another year. A lot of us begin thinking toward spring.

This month's short days are hard on the outdoorsman in us, but those long nights are tailor-made for the gourmet in us. This month is superb for preparing special meals.

Venison roasts, chops, and steaks may begin to become tiring this month, so venison recipes need a drastic change of pace. We have a few to liven up December meals. Also, we have some duck recipes especially for that tough, rare breed of outdoorsman known as the second-season duck hunter.

Duck is a food of extremes. Either people love it, are simply fanatical in their appreciation, or, they simply hate it. Seldom are there any in-betweens. Some of these duck recipes will make converts. But, first, the venison.

VENISON FONDUE

A fondue pot is essential. Inexpensive and simple, it makes a very festive meal. First, gather the following ingredients:

- 2 pounds tender venison, cut into ½-inch cubes, and refrigerated
- 1 cup peanut oil
- ¼ cup butter, preferably clarified
- assorted dips

The venison cubes should be refrigerated a few hours before cooking. The cold cubes are less apt to absorb grease. Peanut oil is ideal, because it does not smoke or spatter as vegetable oil does. The butter need not be clarified, but it is better because it too will be less apt to smoke or spatter.

Heat the oil and butter to 375°, then keep hot over an alcohol burner. Have the cubes arranged on a platter. Two pounds should easily feed four people. If you want to be fancy, arrange the cubes on a bed of lettuce or fresh spinach.

Three minutes cooking time will give you a rare piece of meat. Béarnaise Sauce, Barbecue Sauce, Hot Mustard, or Chili Sauce are good choices of dips, but we prefer simple, melted butter. Serve the fondue with tossed salad, and lots of it, cheeses, French bread, and a good domestic dry red wine.

VENISON STROGANOFF

This is ideal for serving guests. It may be made somewhat ahead, freeing you to make other side dishes, or entertain guests. On top of all that, it is an eloquent meal sure to impress. First, gather the following ingredients:

- 2 pounds cubed venison
- 4 tablespoons flour
- 2–3 tablespoons oil
- 1 teaspoon paprika
- 2 large onions, chopped
- 2 cups beef broth
- salt and pepper to taste
- 1 tablespoon corn starch
- 1 cup sour cream

Put flour into a paper bag, and add cubed venison. Shake the bag, coating the meat thoroughly. Cook in a Dutch oven over a medium heat that has two or three tablespoons oil really sizzling. Sear quickly, then add paprika for color. Stir well, coating the pieces of meat with it. Remove the meat. This whole cooking time should be no more than two minutes.

Add the chopped onions, and cook over a moderate heat until they turn translucent. Do not brown. Replace the meat, then add beef broth. Cover and cook until the meat is tender. If you use a superior cut of venison, this may only be 30 minutes. If it is tough, feel free to simmer it for two hours. Season to taste as it cooks. Remember, if you use canned broth, it is salty anyway, so go easy with additional salt.

Remove the Dutch oven from the heat, let cool for a minute or so, then thicken with corn starch. Just sprinkle in a tablespoon, and beat vigorously with a whip. Place back on a low heat and simmer until the desired thickness is reached.

Again, remove from heat. Add a cup of sour cream and mix thoroughly. Heat the stroganoff again, then serve with egg noodles. Home-made egg noodles really make this meal special. Garnish with chives or parsley flakes, and serve with frenched string beans and slivered almonds, French bread, and a good bottle of Bordeaux, preferably a St. Emilion. A meal guaranteed to bring guests back for seconds, even the bashful ones.

MAINE-STYLE VENISON STEW

Maine-style venison stew must have parsnips! First, gather the following ingredients:

- 1 cup flour
- 1 teaspoon salt
- ½ teaspoon pepper
- 2 pounds cubed venison
- 2–3 tablespoons oil
- 1 large, chopped onion
- 2 potatoes per person, cubed
- 3–4 carrots per person, sliced
- 2 parsnips per person, sliced
- 1 cup string beans (optional)
- 1 cup corn (optional)
- ½ teaspoon poultry seasoning (optional)

In a Dutch oven, preferably cast iron, put two to three tablespoons of oil, and place on a medium heat. Next, put flour, salt, and pepper into a paper bag, and shake vigorously, mixing the ingredients. Put the venison pieces into the bag, and shake again, coating the cubes well. When the oil is hot, add the chopped onions. As soon as they turn translucent, add the pieces of venison, and quickly sear on all sides. While browning, flour will spill from the pieces and begin to brown on the pan's bottom.

As soon as the meat has seared, dump a cup or so of cold water into the pot. It will really sizzle. With a wooden spoon, scrape the flour from the bottom, and stir until the liquid is smooth.

Add potatoes, carrots, parsnips, and optional ingredients, and cover with water. Cook until tender. You may want to serve the stew immediately, or let it simmer half a day, or all day, while you work or play. The flour from the initial browning and the starch from the potatoes will thicken the stew beautifully. Serve with biscuits or popovers, coffee or tea, and cole slaw.

Duck hunters sculling, trying for a little jump shooting. Photo courtesy of Maine Department of Inland Fisheries and Wildlife.

REAL CHILI CON CARNE

Real Chili Con Carne is made with venison, and has absolutely no tomato sauce in it. This dish originated in Texas about 150 years ago. At the time, Texas deer were lean, small, tough little critters. The harsh environment made them leather tough, and something had to be done to make them palatable. Wild desert peppers and wild oregano were plentiful, so pioneers threw chunks of venison, desert peppers, and wild oregano into a stew pot, added water, and cooked the mixture until the meat was tender. Someone got the idea to dump it over pinto beans, and today, Chili Con Carne is relished over the entire continent.

First, gather the following ingredients:

- **3 pounds of cubed venison**
- **¼ cup of oil or rendered beef suet**
- **2–3 tablespoons chili powder**
- **¼ teaspoon cumin**
- **¼ teaspoon garlic powder**
- **1 teaspoon salt**
- **½ teaspoon black pepper**
- **water to cover meat**
- **3–4 chili peppers (optional)**
- **1 grated onion (optional)**

Put the oil or rendered beef suet in a Dutch oven, and place on medium heat. When hot, sear the venison cubes quickly, then add the chili powder, cumin, garlic powder, salt, pepper, and water. When it begins to simmer, you may want to grate an onion into it. We do. Also, some folks like to add the three to four chili peppers now. Cook for two to three hours, or all day over a low heat.

When done, serve over pinto beans with corn bread and beer. Beer is a great beverage with this dish, particularly if the chili is extra hot.

ROAST DUCK—HOT-OVEN METHOD

Wild duck connoisseurs swear by this method. It is strictly for young birds. Older birds must be treated differently. To tell a young bird, look at the tail-feathers. They should end in a V-shaped notch. If tips are pointed or rounded, it probably is an older bird.

After preparing the bird for cooking, wipe with a damp cloth, and rub the inside and out with salt and pepper. Stuff with slices of apples, chunks of celery, quartered onions, and a dozen or so juniper berries. Juniper berries are strictly optional, but it sort of makes you feel like a Euell Gibbons, and does add a slight aromatic touch. This mixture should nearly fill the cavity. It is discarded later, and merely helps flavor the bird. Skewer tightly before roasting.

Rub the outside of the duck liberally with soft butter or olive oil. Next, a choice for a basting sauce. The first one is a quarter of a stick of butter melted and mixed with a teaspoon of Worcestershire Sauce, a teaspoon of lemon juice, and a touch of black pepper. The second choice, the one I prefer, is simply a half-cup of dry red wine.

Whatever one, dribble it on the duck and rub it around, coating the bird. Pop the duck into a preheated 500° oven for 20–30 minutes, depending on the size. Baste quickly but thoroughly every five minutes. The results will be a rare duck, and in many duck connoisseurs' opinion, the only way to eat wild duck.

Serve with wild rice, asparagus, baked squash, French bread, and a good Burgundy.

JOHN KING'S ROAST DUCK

John King, a chef and outdoorsman in Belgrade Lakes, Maine, has a method opposite to the above recipe. He swears by it. He cuts up one orange for each bird. After squeezing the juice from each one, and thoroughly rubbing the bird with it, he puts the orange in the cavity. Then, he slowly cooks the duck(s) at 225° for eight hours.

At this point, the recipe becomes very democratic. Chill the duck(s) for 24 hours, stuff with a favorite stuffing, season to suit taste, then brown in the oven. When the stuffing is done, so is the duck. Serve with rice pilaf, a green veggie, home-made rye bread, and a Bordeaux wine.

ROASTING A SENIOR-CITIZEN DUCK

When you have an older, tougher bird, this is the way to make it into a gourmet dish. Gather the following:

- 1 cup chopped onions
- 1 cup cooked brown rice preferably mixed with wild rice
- 1 cup diced apples, raw
- 3 tablespoons raisins
- salt and pepper to taste
- 2 tablespoons butter

First, simmer the bird in salted water until it is tender. This is usually about 20 minutes per pound. While it simmers, sauté the onions in two tablespoons of butter. When translucent, add to the cooked rice, raw, diced apples, raisins, and salt and pepper to taste. Mix thoroughly, then stuff and skewer the duck.

Rub the outside of the pre-cooked bird with salt, sprinkle with paprika, crisscross liberally with strips of bacon, then pour a cup of claret over the whole bird. Roast at 325° until it has browned well. Baste quickly but thoroughly while it cooks. This should be done about every 10 minutes. The results should be a crisp-skinned bird with a dewy-moist center—the essence of fowl cookery.

Serve with wild rice, a green veggie, French bread, and Bordeaux wine, preferably a St. Emilion. The meal will be memorable.

BROILED DUCK

Such simplicity. Split ducks into halves, baste with soft butter, sprinkle with salt, pepper, and liberal amounts of paprika, and cook six inches from medium coals. Baste frequently with butter. It should be a light basting so there is no flare up from the coals. Serve when done. It should take about an hour. If you turn it and baste every five minutes, the skin will be golden and not black.

Ducks make a meal for royalty. Photo courtesy of Maine Department of Inland Fisheries and Wildlife.

SAUTÉED DUCK BREAST

This recipe is a favorite with Maine guides. It is simplicity in itself. Save the legs, giblets, etc. for soups or stews, and use just the breast.

Clarify enough butter so you will have two to three tablespoons, then add enough olive oil so there is about a quarter inch in the bottom of a frying pan. Bring it to a medium-high heat, then throw in the duck breasts. Make sure they have been patted dry with a paper towel. You want them to brown as quickly as possible, so this initial drying helps.

Remove when cooked to a medium-rare. The taste is similar to venison. Serve with creamy mashed potatoes, a green veggie, biscuits, and a Cabernet Sauvignon.

BRANDIED DUCK BREASTS

At first glance, this recipe seems complicated, but like all great recipes, is simplicity itself. Gather the following ingredients:

- 2–4 **duck breasts**
- ¼ **cup butter**
- ½ **cup flour**
- ½ **teaspoon salt**
- ¼ **teaspoon pepper**
- 1 **cup brandy**
- 1 **cup of wine, red and dry**
- 1 **bay leaf**
- 1 **teaspoon thyme**
- **cooking oil**

Melt butter and let cool until it starts to thicken. While it is cooling, put some flour, salt, and pepper in a paper bag. Shake the bag, mixing the ingredients. Next, thoroughly coat the pieces of duck with the butter, then drop into the paper bag. Shake the bag vigorously, coating the duck well.

Rub a liberal amount of oil on a cold iron frying pan then heat to medium-high. Put the breasts in and brown quickly. This should be about three minutes to a side. Remove from heat, then add half a cup of brandy. Light the brandy with a match.

Be careful. At first, this makes cooks new to the procedure nervous, but eventually, you will delight in this part of the preparation, particularly with an audience present.

When the brandy burns out, add a cup of dry red wine, a crushed bay leaf, a teaspoon of thyme, and then bring to a gentle simmer. Simmer gently for 20–30 minutes, then lift out breasts. Add the other half cup of brandy, then bring to a rolling boil. Scrape the pan's bottom, removing any crusting. Remove from heat and stir vigorously with a whip. Serve the breasts with equal amounts of the sauce. Wild rice, broccoli, French bread, and a good Burgundy make this meal special. A memory to last a lifetime.

QUICHE LORRAINE

Quiche is a great dish for outdoorsmen. It is simple to make, and may be filled with anything from cold partridge breast to crayfish to salmon to wild onions.

The following recipe calls for bacon and onions, and makes an excellent first course before a main course. It does impress guests and family members, and makes you a legend in your own time. Gather the following ingredients:

- 1 **10-inch pie crust**
- 6 **slices of crisply cooked bacon**
- 1 **small to medium onion, finely chopped**
- 4 **eggs, beaten well**
- ½ **teaspoon salt**
- ½ **teaspoon pepper**
- 1 **cup diced cheese, mixture of Cheddar and Swiss**
- 1¼ **cups light cream**

Make a pie crust and line a pie plate with it. Bake the pie shell in a preheated 375° oven for 15 minutes. While it bakes, beat four eggs well, then add salt, pepper, cheese, and cream. Mix it thoroughly.

When the pie shell is done, crumble the six slices of crisp bacon onto the bottom of the shell, then evenly spread the finely chopped onion. Gently pour the egg and cheese mixture into the shell, taking care not to wash the bacon and onions toward the edges. Bake in a 375° oven for 30 minutes. Let stand 10 minutes before cutting, and serve for a first course, or, if a main course, serve with a tossed salad, French bread, and string beans with slivered almonds. A Chablis would be a good choice of wine.

ROAST GOOSE

If someone is lucky enough to score on a Canada goose, it deserves to be served at Christmas. Christmas goose is a dying tradition in this country. Gather the following for stuffing:

- 1 stick of butter
- 2 medium chopped onions
- 4 cups diced apples
- 1 cup of raisins
- chopped, cooked liver of goose
- 1 cup cooked, diced potatoes
- 1 teaspoon salt
- ½ teaspoon pepper
- 1–2 teaspoons poultry seasoning

Place a Dutch oven over a medium-low heat. Melt a stick of butter. When it begins to bubble, add the chopped onions and cook until they first begin to turn translucent. Add the remainder of the ingredients and cook until the apples soften, and the entire mixture is brown. Wipe the cavity of the goose with salt, then stuff and skewer the goose tightly.

Put the goose on a rack, cover with aluminum foil, and roast in a preheated 375° oven for about 2–2½ hours. Remove the foil, prick the bird in several places with a fork, then return to the oven without the foil, and cook until the skin is crisp and brown, about 30–45 minutes. The results will be a golden skin with dewy-moist center—the essence of cookery. Canada goose is food fit for the gods, so serve a superior bottle of French Burgundy, preferably a heavy Burgundy such as a Chambertin or Nuits-Saint-Georges.

Wild rice is a must with Canada goose. Baked squash, asparagus, and French bread will make a meal with a memory to last a lifetime.

Eat, drink, and relish the season. A year has slid by...much too quickly. With luck and patience and skill, nature's bounty had been good to us. Living close to the Earth, we know where our meals have come, and have eaten them the way we should...with reverence.

Chapter 14
The Wheat Connection

It's lunchtime. It may be beside a trout stream in May, or a bird covert in October. A friend sets a large wedge of cheese between you, then hands over a knife. Cheese is rather unexciting, just something to ease hunger pangs, and you might say, "Thanks, I'll try a piece."

Your friend reaches into his rucksack, and pulls out a bottle of wine, a couple of glasses, and a large loaf of home-made bread, freshly baked with a golden, crusty outside and soft, yeasty inside, and that small lunch begins to take on epoch proportions.

Any meal becomes suddenly special with home-made bread. The tradition is there. For millennia, monumental decisions have transpired around a a loaf of bread, changing the history of the world. In some cultures, bread is symbolic of food itself. However, beyond all that, home-baked bread makes the meal. Coquilles St. Jacques and rice pilaf, steak and baked potatoes, venison stew, no matter how eloquent or plain, bread enhances the feast.

FRENCH BREAD

There is just something about French bread. It has such snob appeal, elevating the humblest meal to gourmet heights. However, it is the easiest yeast bread to make. The following recipe requires no kneading, and the ingredients are basic. You need just water, yeast, sugar, salt, and flour. What could be easier? And, the results will be perfect French bread.

First, fill a heavy, crock bowl with hot water, and let stand while you gather the following ingredients:

> **2 cups warm water**
> **1 package dry yeast**
> **1 tablespoon sugar**
> **1½ teaspoons salt**
> **4½–5 cups unsifted flour, preferably unbleached flour**
> **cornmeal for dusting baking sheet**

Dump the hot water from the bowl, leaving you with a prewarmed mixing bowl. Add two cups of lukewarm water. To tell the proper temperature for the yeast, pour some of the water on the inside of your wrist. If it feels either too warm or too cool, try again. If you are unable to feel the water because it is the same as your body temperature, it is perfect.

Sprinkle in the yeast, and stir with a wooden spoon until it dissolves. Add the sugar and mix thoroughly. Let the yeast mixture sit for at least three minutes, then add the salt.

You are now ready for the flour. Add it one cup at a time, and beat it with a wooden spoon. Add enough flour to make a smooth dough. If the dough is too wet, it will cause problems later. Since the loaves will sit on a baking sheet with nothing to hold in the sides, wet dough will spread out as it rises. A heavier, drier dough will rise up more than out.

Clean the mixing bowl, then lightly grease. Put the dough in, and cover with a damp, linen cloth. Remember, do not knead it. Let the dough double in size, then punch it down. We always let the dough rise again before making the loaves. The finished product will be consistently better.

After it has risen twice, turn it onto a floured board and let it stand for 10 minutes, then divide in half. Roll one of these dough balls into an oblong shape one-quarter inch thick. It will be almost rectangular. Now, fold it like a business letter. Fold one-third of the dough toward the center, then fold the other third over it. Pinch down the seams and ends, sealing the loaf. Lay it on a baking sheet that has been sprinkled with cornmeal.

Prepare the other dough ball in the same manner, and lay it beside the first one. Gently wash excess flour from the loaves with lukewarm water. Score diagonally with a sharp knife. This keep the loaves from splitting while cooking. Cover with a damp cloth, and let the loaves double in size.

Put a pan of water in the oven, then preheat to 400°. When the loaves have doubled in size, place in the oven for 40 minutes, or more. During the baking time, baste the loaves with cold water about every 10 minutes. This will make them delightfully crusty. When done, knock excess cornmeal from them, and set loaves on wire racks.

BASIC WHITE BREAD

Before technology enabled mass production of white flour, white bread was only in the realm of the aristocracy and clergy. A veritable luxury. This is a simple recipe. First, gather the following ingredients:

- ¼ **cup warm water**
- 1 **package dry yeast**
- 1 **cup milk**
- 2 **tablespoons butter, shortening, or margarine**
- 2 **tablespoons sugar**
- 1½ **teaspoons salt**
- 1 **cup warm water**
- 6 **cups unsifted flour**

In a small, prewarmed bowl, add one-quarter of a cup of warm water. Test the temperature on your wrist. Sprinkle yeast into the bowl, and stir to dissolve. Preparing the yeast now gives it an opportunity to sit awhile.

Next, over a medium-low heat, place a saucepan with a cup of milk, two tablespoons of sugar, and a teaspoon-and-a-half of salt. Stir to dissolve dry ingredients. Add the butter, shortening, or margarine. As soon as it melts and the milk begins to steam, remove from the heat. Pour this mixture into a prewarmed mixing bowl, preferably a heavy crock one.

As soon as it cools to about body temperature, add two cups of flour, and stir to blend. Then, add the cup of warm water and yeast, and stir again, blend it well. You may want to use a whip or electric beater. When done, there should be bubbles in the batter.

Now, add the additional four cups. Do it one cup at a time, and stir it with a wooden spoon. Beat until the dough is smooth. Roll it onto a floured board, grease the palms of your hand, then knead until it is a smooth ball. Clean the mixing bowl with warm water, grease well with shortening, then place the dough in it. Brush oil or melted shortening onto the dough, cover with a linen towel, and place in a warm, draft-free place.

When the dough has doubled in size, and dents remain in it when you poke it with your finger, punch it down. Turn the dough over in the bowl, cover with a damp linen towel, and let rise again. Roll it onto a floured board, cut in half, then form two balls. Cover with a linen towel, and let stand for 10 minutes.

Form two loaves and put into 9x5x3-inch loaf pans. Cover again and wait until dough begins to rise above the pans. Place in a preheated 400° oven for 40–50 minutes.

RYE BREAD

This is a foolproof rye bread recipe, and excellent for camp cooking. Buttermilk is used, and this lasts longer than regular milk. First, gather the following ingredients:

- ¼ cup warm water
- 1 package dry yeast
- 1 cup buttermilk
- ¼ cup dark molasses
- 1½ teaspoons salt
- 2 tablespoons caraway seeds
- 2 tablespoons shortening
- 1 cup warm water
- 3 cups sifted white flour
- 3 cups sifted rye flour

Put a quarter cup of warm water into a prewarmed soup bowl. Test the temperature of the water on your wrist. Sprinkle the yeast in and stir to dissolve. Make certain the yeast has dissolved thoroughly.

Put a saucepan over a moderate heat, and add the buttermilk, molasses, salt, and caraway seeds. Stir thoroughly with a whip, mixing the ingredients, particularly the molasses, really well. Then, add two tablespoons of shortening. When the shortening melts and the buttermilk begins to steam a little, remove from heat. Be careful. Buttermilk curdles easily. Put the buttermilk mixture in a prewarmed mixing bowl. When it cools to body temperature, add two cups of flour, and mix. Then, add a cup of warm water, and beat with a whip or electric beater until bubbles form in the batter. Stir in the yeast mixture, and blend thoroughly.

Add the additional four cups of flour one cup at a time. Stir with a wooden spoon until the dough is somewhat smooth, then place on a well-floured board for a few minutes. Clean the mixing bowl with warm water, then dry and grease with shortening.

Grease your hands heavily with shortening before kneading. The dough is sticky because of the molasses. Knead the dough until it becomes smooth, then place it in the greased bowl. Brush oil or melted shortening on top, cover with a linen towel that has been dampened, then place bowl in warm, draft-free spot. When the dough doubles in size, punch down, turn over in bowl, brush again with oil or shortening, then let rise again.

Now, roll it onto a floured board and cover with cloth. Let it stand for 10 minutes. Cut into equal halves, and form into round loaves. Sort of pinch the bottoms together so they resemble giant mushroom caps. If the dough is too wet, the loaves will spread out as they rise. If the dough is somewhat dry, they will rise beautifully. Cover, and let rise again.

Place in a preheated 400° oven, and cook for 50 minutes, or until the bottoms sound hollow when you thump them. If your oven begins to burn the top, brush shortening or butter on. The finished product is fantastic rye bread.

POPOVERS

Popovers are simple to make, difficult to ruin, and very festive. They will make you a legend in your own time, or at least, in your family where it really counts. Gather the following ingredients:

- **4 eggs**
- **1 teaspoon salt**
- **2 cups milk**
- **2 cups flour**
- **2 tablespoons melted butter**

With a high-speed mixer, beat the eggs and salt until the mixture is light in consistency. Add a half cup of milk and two cups of flour. Beat mixture until the flour is moist. Gradually dribble in the remainder of the milk. Continue beating the batter until it is smooth. Add the melted butter and thoroughly blend. Grease a muffin tin quite heavily, and pour batter into each cup, filling three-quarters full. Bake for 40 minutes at 425°. Don't peek. It may make them fall. Serve pipin' hot with lots of butter.

BISCUITS

This is absolutely the best biscuit recipe we have ever encountered, making biscuits extra light and high. It is actually the recipe on the back of a Bakewell Cream box, only the recipe is cut in half, so the credit should go to the Byron H. Smith & Company of Bangor, Maine.

First, gather the following ingredients:

- **2 cups flour**
- **2 teaspoons Bakewell Cream**
- **1 teaspoon soda**
- **½ teaspoon salt**
- **¼ cup shortening**
- **¾ cup cold milk**

Mix and sift dry ingredients into a mixing bowl. Add the quarter cup of shortening, and cut it in with a pastry blender or fork. Add milk. Sour milk works great, but sweet milk is fine also. Dump the milk in all at once, and stir quickly with a wooden spoon. Knead right in the bowl just a half dozen times. Don't overdo it. Then, turn dough onto floured board.

Roll to a half-inch thickness, and cut with a biscuit cutter. A simple can with both ends cut out is great. It does not compress the dough as many commercial cutters do. Place biscuits into a well-greased pan. If you place them close together, the sides will be soft when done. If you space them, the sides will be brown and crispy. Put a thin pad of butter or a half-teaspoon milk on top of each one. If you let them sit for 10–15 minutes, they will begin to rise, and the finished product will be a higher biscuit.

Whether you let them rise a little, or put them into the oven immediately, cook them in a preheated 475° oven for five minutes. Turn the heat off, and leave until golden brown, about five to ten minutes. Serve hot with lots and lots of butter.

BUTTERMILK BISCUITS

Use the above recipe, but substitute buttermilk for regular milk. If the buttermilk is especially thick it may be necessary to add slightly more. Use just enough so the dough leaves the sides of the bowl. Too much liquid makes the dough sticky; too little and it's dry. Buttermilk adds a delightful flavor, rich in tradition.

PANCAKES

This a great recipe that may be altered slightly to achieve different results. First, gather the following ingredients:

- 1 cup flour
- 1 teaspoon baking soda
- 1 teaspoon baking powder
- ¼ teaspoon salt
- 1 egg
- 1½ cups milk
- 1 tablespoon melted butter

If you use a half cup of rye flour and a half cup of white flour, the pancakes will taste like buckwheat pancakes. In short, delicious.

Put the cup of unsifted flour into a mixing bowl, then add baking soda, baking powder, and salt. Mix ingredients thoroughly. Next, in a small bowl, beat an egg, then add milk. Sour milk makes a great pancake, impressing family and friends. Mix the milk and egg. Add this mixture to the dry ingredients, and mix with a minimum of stirring. This is the secret to a light pancake. Leave lumps—just mix it enough to make a batter. Stir in the melted butter.

Cook on a well-greased griddle. Sprinkle a drop or two of water on the griddle before cooking. If the droplets skitter around, the heat is perfect.

With one-and-a-half cups of milk, the batter is thin; consequently, the pancake is thin and light like a crêpe. If you like thicker pancakes, use one cup of milk.

Fruits such as blueberries are a popular addition to pancake batter. However, try this interesting addition. Use whole-kernel corn. Sounds silly! However, it makes a rich pancake, and may start a family tradition.

CORNMEAL PANCAKES

This makes hearty pancakes for a man-sized breakfast. Gather the following ingredients:

- ½ cup powdered milk
- 1½ cups cornmeal
- 1 teaspoon salt
- 1 teaspoon baking powder
- 1½ cups milk, preferably sour
- 2 egg whites
- 2 tablespoons corn oil

Mix the powdered milk, cornmeal, salt, and baking powder in a mixing bowl, then add milk and corn oil. Mix the ingredients, then fold in two, well-beaten egg whites. Fold gently. Cook in oil in a 350° skillet. This makes a delicious pancake, rich and very filling, the kind of breakfast that sticks with you through a strenuous morning of hunting, fishing, or working.

TRADITIONAL PIE CRUST

This is a sure-fire recipe for superior, flaky pie crust. Gather the following ingredients:

- 2 cups sifted flour
- 1 teaspoon salt
- ⅔ cup of shortening
- 5–7 tablespoons ice water

Mix the sifted flour and salt thoroughly. Cut shortening into the flour with a pastry cutter until shortening makes tiny balls the size of pebbles. Stop blending then. Don't over do this cutting process. Add water a tablespoon at a time, and mix until you can make a heavy ball of dough. Do not use more than seven tablespoons water.

Roll ball in wax paper and refrigerate for at least an hour. Three would be even better because this pastry dough rolls so much better when it is cold. When rolling, use a floured board. Cut the ball in half, and roll one for the bottom of the pie, and one for the top crust.

HOMEMADE NOODLES

Homemade noodles are superior to the boxed variety found in supermarkets. Once you try this recipe, a family tradition will be born. Gather the following ingredients:

- **2 cups unsifted flour**
- **½ teaspoon salt**
- **2 eggs (unbeaten)**
- **1–4 tablespoons water**

In a mixing bowl, mix the flour and salt thoroughly, then form a well in the center. Add the unbeaten eggs and one tablespoon water. With a wooden spoon, beat the eggs and water, and slowly add flour to the liquid. You may keep adding one tablespoon of water until you have used four, but do not use more than four—no matter how dry the dough may seem. A secret to good homemade noodles is to use as little water as possible. If you have the patience, keep working with just one tablespoon of water.

After a stiff dough forms, one that easily pulls away from the bowl, begin to knead. Knead for 10 minutes, then lay a wet towel over the bowl, and let stand for one-half hour.

On a floured board, place the dough and roll out with a rolling pin. If you are making egg noodles, a favorite with venison stroganoff, rabbit and noodles, or any similar dish, roll as thin as possible. It should be almost transparent. If you are making lasagna noodles, they need not be as thin. Cut into strips and lay on bread racks to dry completely.

When ready to cook, add to salted, boiling water with a touch of oil, and cook eight minutes, or until tender. Homemade foods are always superior, and homemade noodles are no exception.

CORN BREAD

This country grew up eating corn bread. Here is a fine recipe that makes corn bread like grandma used to. It does not crumble and fall apart when buttered. Gather the following ingredients:

- 1 cup sifted flour (you may want to have half white flour; half whole wheat. It makes a browner bread)
- 1 cup sifted cornmeal
- ¼ cup white sugar
- 3 teaspoons baking powder
- ¾ teaspoon salt
- 1 cup buttermilk (regular will work)
- 1 egg
- ¼ cup melted lard, or shortening

Sift the flour and cornmeal, then measure out a cup of each. If you use one-half cup of white flour, and one-half cup of whole wheat flour, the results will be a browner bread. Next, add a quarter cup sugar, three teaspoons baking powder, three-quarter teaspoon salt, and mix thoroughly. Sift all the ingredients.

Next, in the mixing bowl, add a cup of milk, preferably buttermilk. Buttermilk is great to have around the house for baking. A fresh quart will last a month before souring. Next, add the egg. Beat the mixture well, then add the quarter cup of melted lard. Make sure it has cooled somewhat before adding or it will curdle the buttermilk. Mix this liquid thoroughly.

Add the sifted dry ingredients, and mix just enough to make a damp dough. Do no overmix this batter. It is meant to be dampened just enough to pour into a well-greased 8x8 pan, or a round cake pan.

Bake in a preheated 400° oven for 30 minutes, then serve pipin' hot with lots and lots of butter. Homemade corn bread is food fit for the gods.

Homemade bread. It takes a little extra time, but the appreciation will be of epoch proportions. Any meal becomes an epicurean delight, a healthful one.

MY OWN COOKING WILD RECIPES

MY OWN COOKING WILD RECIPES

MY OWN COOKING WILD RECIPES

INDEX

A

Asparagus, boiled 78
   creamed asparagus 78

B

Baked Fish, bass 86
   lake trout (togue) 60
   old favorite 120
   pickerel 23
   salmon 71
   striper a la tomatoes 116-117
Bass, bass chowder 88
   bass salad 86
   baked bass 88
   deep-fried bass 85
   rolled-stuffed filets 88-89
   sauteed bass 86
Bear, bear chops 130
   bear fat 130
   bear roast 129
   bear stew 128
   grilled bear ribs 129
   marinated bear roast 129-130
Bluefish, grilled steaks 115-116
Bread, basic white bread 189-190
   biscuits 192
   buttermilk biscuits 194
   corn bread 198
   cornmeal pancakes 195
   French bread 188
   noodles (homemade) 197
   pie crust (traditional) 195
   pancakes 194
   popovers 191-192
   rye bread 190-191
Broth, clear poultry 151
Butter, clarified 10

C

Carrots, brandied 131
   brandied wild carrots 132
   cattails, boiled cat-tail flowers ... 94
   sauteed cat-tail stems 94
   steamed cat-tail stems 94
Chile con carne 179
Chowders, bass 20-21
   clam 102
   cusk 20-21
   flounder 20-21
   haddock 20-21
   hornpout 20-21
   perch 20-21
   pickerel 20-21
   pollock 20-21
   salmon 20-21
   sunfish 20-21
   trout 57

Clams, broiled 104
   clam cakes 106
   clam chowder 102
   fried clams 104
   steamed clams 100
Cleaning fish and game, big-game .. 9
   fish 10
   small game 7-8
   upland birds 8-9
   waterfowl 9
Coquille St. Jacques 28-29
Corn bread 198
Corn-on-the-cob 122-124
Crayfish, boiled in beer 107-108
   potted crayfish 121
   quiche 122

D

Dandelion, boiled 65
   Maine-style 65-66
Duck, brandied duck breasts .. 183-184
   broiled duck 181
   John King's roast duck 180
   roast duck—hot-oven method 180
   roasting senior-citizen duck 181
   sauteed duck breast 183

E

Eels, coal-broiled eels 90
   eels in beer 90
   grilled eels 89
Eggs, boiled 44
   fried 44
   omelette 42-43
   scrambled 44
   shirred eggs with ham 43

F

Fiddleheads, boiled or steamed 64
   creamed fiddleheads on toast 79
   identification 64
   fiddlehead salad 79
Filets, deep-fried bass 85
   deep-fried hornpout 92
   grilled sole 117
   grilled striper in Italian dressing . 116
   oven-fried 120
   poached in white wine 118
   rolled-stuffed 88-89
Fondue 176
French fries 33
Frog's legs, sauteed 108

G

Garlic clove cookery 7
Goose, roasted 185
Gravy basics 6-7

Grouse, cold roast grouse 147
   Eustis grouse 147
   plum wine grouse 145
   roasted grouse 144-145

H

Halibut, baked, stuffed 39
Hasenpfeffer 37
Homefries, Coopers Mills-style 47
   Maine-style 47
   Massachusetts-style 48
   Southern-style 48
   Western-style 49
Hornpout, chowder 20-21
   deep-fried 92

J

Jugged hare 15

K

Kabobs, beef 135
   lamb 135
   moose 135
   venison 135
Kitchen utensils 5-6

L

Liver, and onions 168-169

M

Mackerel, grilled 115
   mustard-butter grilled 115
Mint (wild), identification 62
   with lake trout 62
Moose,
   Canadian style 132
   kabobs 135-136
   lazy man's pot roast 132
   marinated roast 135
   marinated steak 132
   pan-fried steak 134
   roast 134
   stew 132
Mushroom, baked stuffed 139
   creamed on toast 81
   marinated 137
   morels (identification) 79
   sauteed mushrooms, green
      peppers, and onions 172
   sauteing 81
   stuffing 71

O

Omelette 42-43

P

Peas (fresh), boiled 100

Perch, chowder 20-21
   fried 23
Pheasant, au vin 150-152
   fricasseed 150
   in cream 153
   in sour cream 152-153
   larded, roasted 149
   roasted 149
Poached Fish, blue trout 63
   eels in beer 90
   filets in white wine 118
   salmon 74
   trout 58
Potatoes, buttered-parsleyed 98
   cold mashed potato salad 124
   french fries 33
   German potato salad 131
   homefries 47-49
   scalloped 76
   Swedish baked 164
   Thomas Jefferson boiled 98

Q

Quiche, crayfish 122
   Lorraine 184

R

Rabbit, fricasseed 19
   fried 18
   hasenpfeffer 37
   jugged hare 15
   over noodles 36
   pie 17
   stew 16
Ribs, barbecued 107
   barbecued bear 129
   barbecued deer 107
   barbecued spare ribs 107
Rice, for baked stuffed tomatoes ... 158
   pilaf 30
   wild (boiled) 140-141
   wild (identification) 140
   wild mixed with brown rice 140

S

Salmon, baked 71
   broiled 72
   Fourth of July salmon 98
   loaf 75
   planked 74
   poached 74
   sauteed 72
Sauces, barbecue (for meats) 106
   barbecue (for fish) 117
   meuniere 58
   mornay 28-29
   tomato sauce for fish 116
   white 78
Scallops, broiled 31
   Coquille St. Jacques 28-29

Seafood,
   bluefish, grilled steaks 115-116
   clams, broiled 104
      cakes...................... 106
      chowder 102
      fried 104
      steamed 100
   halibut, baked, stuffed 39
   fish chowder 20-21
   filets, grilled sole.............. 117
   grilled striper in Italian dressing 116
      oven-fried.................. 120
      poached in white wine 118
   mackerel, grilled 115
      mustard-butter grilled 115
   scallops, broiled 31
      Coquille St. Jacques 28-29
   shrimp, boiled in shell........... 32
      boiled without shell 32
      deep-fried.................. 33
      potted 121
   sole, grilled 117-118
   striped bass, baked a la
      tomato 116-117
      grilled in Italian dressing 116
Seasoning cast iron utensils 4-5
Shrimp, boiled in shell 32
   boiled without shell 32
   deep-fried 33
   potted 121
Sole, grilled 117-118
Soup, cold blackberry............. 122
   cold raspberry 110
   cold strawberry 92
Squash, baked 137
   perfect mashed 136
   summer squash casserole 109
Squirrel, camp-style 156
   fricasseed.................... 156
   fried 155
   over noodled 156
   pie 155
   stew 155
Striped bass, baked
   a la tomatoes 116-117
   grilled in Italian dressing 116
Stroganoff.................. 176-177
Stuffing, for bass 86
   for lake trout (togue) 60
   for mushrooms................ 139
   gourmet seafood 88
   mushroom for fish 71
   poultry bread stuffing 144
Substituting main ingredients 6
Sumacade 125

T

Tomatoes, grilled 136
   baked stuffed 158
Trout, baked lake trout (togue) 60
   blue trout 63
   grilled trout 57
   Maine-style trout 56
   old favorite baked fish.......... 120
   oven-fried trout 56
   poached trout 58
   sauteed trout 56
   spitted trout 57
   trout chowder 57
   truites a la meuniere 58
   wilderness lake trout
      (togue) with mint 62

V

Vegetables,
   asparagus, boiled.............. 78
      creamed on toast 78
   carrots, brandied 131
      brandied wild 132
   cattails, boiled flowers 94
      sauteed stems 94
      steamed stems 94
   corn, on-the-cob 122-124
   dandelions, boiled 65
      Maine-style 65-66
   fiddleheads, boiled or steamed ... 64
      creamed on toast 79
      identification 64
      salad 79
   mint, identification 62
      with lake trout 62
   mushrooms
      baked and stuffed 139
      creamed on toast 81
      marinated 137
      morels 79
      sauteing 81
      sauteed
      mushrooms, green peppers,
         and onions.............. 172
      stuffing for fish 71
   peas (fresh), boiled 100
   potatoes,
      buttered-parsleyed 98
      cold mashed potato salad 124
      french fried 33
      German potato casserole 131
      homefries................. 47-49
      scalloped 76
      Swedish baked 164
      Thomas Jefferson
         boiled potato 98
   squash, baked 137
      perfect mashed 136
      summer squash casserole...... 109
   tomatoes, grilled 136
      baked stuffed 158
Venison, beer pot roast,
   Canadian style 51
   bourguignon 169-171
   breaded cutlet 166
   broiled chops 163
   broiled steaks 162-163
   chile con carne................ 179

deer burger 52
Diane 168
fondue 176
heart....................... 171
kabobs 135-136
lazy man's pot roast 50
liver and onions 168-169
Maine-style stew.......... 177-178
our favorite steak recipe 162
pan-broiled 171
roast 163-164
stroganoff 176-177
stuffed roast 164

W

Woodchuck, braised in wine 66-67
Woodcock, bacon 149
  medallion of woodcock 148
  sauteed 148
  baked in cream 148